It's Just Like Poker
A Spiritual Guide to Playing the Cards Life Deals You

Dr. Constance Santego

Maximillian Enterprises
Kelowna, BC

It's Just Like Poker: A Spiritual Guide to Playing the Cards Life Deals You

Copyright © 2025 by Constance Santego.

Copy Editor & Interior Design: Constance Santego
Book Layout: ©2017 BookDesignTemplates.com

Ordering Information:
Quantity sales. Special discounts are available on quantity purchases by corporations, associations, and others. Contact the "Special Sales Department" at the address below for details.

Trade Paperback ISBN: 978-1-990062-71-1
eBook ISBN 978-1-990062-72-8
Created and published In Canada. Printed and bound in the United States of America

First Edition
Published by Maximillian Enterprises
Kelowna, BC
Canada
www.constancesantego.ca

ALSO BY DR. CONSTANCE SANTEGO

NOVELS

Illegitimate Grace

Okanagan Trilogy:

Beneath the Vineyards
Under the Okanagan Sun
Guardian of the Lake

The Nine Spiritual Gifts Series:
Journey of a Soul – (Vol 1 Michael)
Language of a Soul – (Vol 2 Gabriel)
Prophecy of a Soul – (Vol 3 Bath Kol)
Healing of a Soul – (Vol 4 Raphael)
Miracles of a Soul – (Vol 5 Hamied)
Knowledge of a Soul – (Vol 6 Raziel)
Wisdom of a Soul – (Vol 7 Uriel)
Faith of a Soul – (Vol 8 Pistis Sophia)

NONFICTION

The Intuitive Life, The Gift Of Prophecy, Third Edition
Fairy Tales, Dreams And Reality… Where Are You On Your Path? Second Edition
Your Persona… The Mask You Wear
Archangel Michael's Soul Retrieval Guide
Tesla And The Future Of Energy Medicine
Beyond Tesla: *Advancing The Science Of Energy Healing*
Tesla's Code: *Mastering Energy, Frequency, And Creative Power*
Beyond the Mind: *Harnessing the Power of Astral Projection for Creative Awakening*
Bend, Don't Break: *Finding Your Way Back to Abundance*
Ring Therapy: *A Guide to Healing and Balance*
Ring Therapy Pocket Guide
Floraopathy™: *The Art and Science of Vibrational Healing with Essential Oils*
Dear Older Me: *A Memoir… of Sorts*

REIKI WISDOM, SERIES:

Angelic Lifestyle, a Vibrant Lifestyle
Angelic Lifestyle 42-Day Energy Cleanse
Reiki and the Power of The Joint Points: *Unlocking Energy Pathways for Healing* (Vol I)
Reiki and Karmic Healing: *Releasing Patterns From Past Lives* (Vol II)
Reiki and the Five Elements (Vol III)
Secrets of a Healer, Magic Of Reiki
The Reiki Master's Manual

SECRETS OF A HEALER, SERIES:

Magic Of Aromatherapy (Vol I)
Magic Of Reflexology (Vol II)
Magic Of The Gifts (Vol III)
Magic Of Muscle Testing (Vol IV)
Magic Of Iridology (Vol V)
Magic Of Massage (Vol VI)
Magic Of Hypnotherapy (Vol VII)
Magic Of Reiki (Vol VIII)
Magic Of Advanced Aromatherapy (Vol IX)
Magic Of Esthetics (Vol X)
The Reiki Master's Manual (Vol XI)

ADULT COLORING JOURNALS

SERIES-ZEN COLORING:
Quantum Energy and Mindful Living Journal (Vol 1)
Reiki Energy Journal (Vol 2)
Nine Spiritual Gifts Journal (Vol 3)
I Forgive Journal (Vol 4)

FOR CHILDREN
I am Big Tonight. I Don't Need the Light

COOKBOOK
My Favorite Recipes, with a Hint of Giggle

BUISNESS
Scaling Beyond 6 Figures: *Strategies For Health & Wellness Professionals*
How To Use Chatgpt For Authors: From Idea To Published Book

Dedication to

To everyone who's ever felt like life dealt them a losing hand—
This book is for you. May you find the courage to stay at the table, trust your gut, and play again.

Life's a game. The deck is always shuffling.
But even when the odds seem stacked against you…
Shift happens—so create your own magic.

—Dr. Constance Santego

Preface

Life doesn't come with a rulebook, but if it did, I imagine it would read a lot like poker.
Some days you're dealt a winning hand. Other days? Total garbage.
You make your bets, read the room, trust your instincts—and sometimes, despite your best efforts, you still lose.

And yet, you keep playing.

This book was born out of those moments in life that feel unfair, unpredictable, or downright magical. Over the years, I've come to realize that what matters most isn't the cards we're dealt—it's how we *play* them. The patience we show. The intuition we trust. The risks we take. The grace with which we walk away or go all in.

It's Just Like Poker is not about the game itself, but about the game *behind* the game—the deeper metaphors hidden in everyday moments. The hands we play mirror our relationships, our dreams, our doubts, our healing, and our faith.

This book is for the intuitive souls, the quiet warriors, the ones who feel like life is trying to teach them something just beyond the surface. It's for those who've bluffed their way through tough times, folded when they had to, and still believed in miracles when the river card turned.

May this book remind you that even when the table feels tilted and the odds seem against you… there's always a higher wisdom at play.

Take a deep breath.
Pick up your hand.
And remember:
You were born to play.

—Dr. Constance Santego

"Life doesn't ask you to control the cards—only to play them with wisdom, courage, and grace."

♠ Texas Hold'em 101: The Game Behind the Metaphor

Before we dive into the wisdom within the cards, here's a quick breakdown of how Texas Hold'em works—because life, like poker, has rules, rhythms, and risks.

The Basics:

Each player is dealt two private cards (called *hole cards*). Then, five *community cards* are revealed face-up in the center of the table. Players make the best five-card hand using any combination of their hole cards and the community cards.

The Four Betting Rounds:

1. Pre-Flop: After everyone receives two cards, the first round of betting begins.
2. The Flop: Three community cards are revealed. Second betting round.
3. The Turn: A fourth community card is revealed. Third betting round.
4. The River: The fifth and final community card is revealed. Final bets are placed.

At the end, if more than one player remains, there's a showdown to determine the winner.

The Blinds:

To keep the game moving, two players must post forced bets:

- Small Blind: Half the minimum bet
- Big Blind: Full minimum bet

These rotate around the table so everyone contributes.

Your Choices Each Round:

- Fold: Surrender your cards and exit the hand
- Call: Match the current bet
- Raise: Increase the bet
- Check: Pass without betting (only allowed if no one has raised)

Hand Rankings (High to Low):

1. Royal Flush: A–K–Q–J–10, all the same suit
2. Straight Flush: Five cards in sequence, same suit
3. Four of a Kind: Four cards of the same value
4. Full House: Three of a kind + a pair
5. Flush: Five cards of the same suit
6. Straight: Five cards in sequence (any suit)
7. Three of a Kind
8. Two Pair
9. One Pair
10. High Card

The Wisdom in the Game:

Poker isn't just about the cards—it's about reading people, managing risk, and trusting your gut. It's a dance between strategy and surrender—a game of decisions, not just luck.

This is why poker makes such a powerful metaphor for life. You won't always know what's coming. You won't control the hand you're dealt. But you can still play with presence, intuition, and power.

And that's what this book is about.

What's a Vignette—And Why It Matters in This Book

As you read through each chapter, you'll notice a short scene near the end—a brief moment in someone's life or at the poker table. These are called vignettes.

A vignette isn't a full story. There's no long plot or dramatic arc. Instead, it's like a snapshot. A glimpse into a situation. A single hand played. A decision made in the heat of the moment.

But here's the magic:
In just a few lines, a vignette can show you more than pages of explanation. It lets you *feel* the lesson, not just read about it.

Whether it's a player walking away from the table at just the right time…
Or someone holding nothing in their hand, but everything in their gut…
These moments are here to help you *see* yourself in the game—and in life.

Some are fictional. Some are real. But all are chosen to stir something in you.

So as you turn the pages, don't just look for the lesson.
Enter the scene. Picture it. Feel it. Then ask yourself: What would I do in that moment?

Because this book isn't just about poker.
It's about *your game*. Your story. Your next move.

And these vignettes?
They're the mirror.

Contents

"Life is not always a matter of holding good cards, but sometimes, playing a poor hand well."

— Jack London

It's Just Like Poker

A Spiritual Guide to Playing the Cards Life Deals You

Introduction: Life at the Table

Life is a table we all sit at—some of us by choice, others by circumstance. From the moment we arrive, the cards begin to fall. Some are dealt privilege, health, or early love. Others receive pain, loss, or limitation. And while the game might look different for everyone, the one thing we all have in common is this:

**We don't control the hand we're dealt…
but we do control how we play it.**

This book isn't about poker in the traditional sense. It's about the deeper game beneath the surface—the spiritual game of life. The one where timing matters, but so does patience. Where bluffing can be confidence, or fear in disguise. Where folding isn't failure, but wisdom. Where sometimes you win by staying in… and sometimes, by letting go.

At the heart of this game is one essential truth: your power lies not in what happens to you, but in how you respond.

Like poker, life teaches us lessons in every round. It sharpens our intuition. It humbles us with losses and lifts us with sudden wins. It reminds us that luck is real—but so is alignment. When you trust your gut, stay present, and learn from the players around you, magic happens.

There will be days when the river card breaks your heart. There will be days when you win with the worst hand at the table. And in those moments, you'll discover something essential: the game was never just about the cards. It was about you.

So take a breath. Sit down with your whole heart. Pick up the hand life gave you.
This isn't just poker.
This is your transformation in motion.

Pull Up a Chair

You don't need to know the rules of poker to understand this
book—
you just need to have lived a little.

If you've ever felt like life handed you a losing hand…
If you've ever trusted your gut and won big…
If you've ever had to fold and walk away with your head held
high…
Then you've already played.

So pull up a chair.
The cards are being dealt.
This table? It's yours too.

Let's begin.

The Symbolism of the Game

Poker isn't just a game of cards. It's a reflection of life itself.

Each hand begins with a deal—random, unpredictable, and often unfair. You don't choose your cards. You're simply handed what you're handed, just like you didn't choose your family, your genetics, or the timing of your challenges.

From there, the game unfolds. You place your bets—just as you do in life when you commit to a relationship, a job, a dream, or a leap of faith. Sometimes you bluff—masking your fear or pain behind a smile. Other times, you play your hand honestly and boldly, trusting that it's enough.

There's strategy, yes. But there's also luck. Intuition. Timing. And the art of reading the energy in the room. You win not just with the best hand—but by playing with awareness, courage, and wisdom.

In poker, as in life, there are no guarantees.
But there *are* lessons.
And that's what this book is about.

The Spiritual Game

At first glance, poker may seem like a game of chance. But look deeper, and you'll find it mirrors the most profound aspects of our inner journey.

Every decision at the table asks:

Do you trust yourself?
Can you sit with uncertainty?
Will you act with courage—or fear?

These are the same questions we face in life, especially on the path of spiritual growth. Each hand becomes a test of faith, patience, intuition, and self-awareness. The more you play, the more you realize that winning isn't about controlling the outcome—it's about mastering your response.

In personal development, we talk about knowing your worth, managing emotions, setting boundaries, trusting your instincts, and surrendering to what is.
Isn't that the same as reading your cards, staying calm in high-stakes moments, and knowing when to fold or go all in?

The table becomes your teacher.
The game becomes your guide.
And the hand you're holding?
It's not just a challenge—it's your next invitation to grow.

This book is for those ready to play with presence, evolve with every hand, and discover the soul behind the strategy.

Part I:
The Deal – What Life Hands You

Suit: Spades
Symbolism: Wisdom, intellect, challenge, and transformation.

Chapter 1: The Cards You're Dealt

None of us gets to shuffle the deck we're born into.

Some arrive with aces—loving families, stable homes, good health, and early opportunities. Others start with a losing hand—abuse, poverty, chronic illness, or invisible wounds passed down through generations. We don't choose these first cards. They're simply dealt to us.

Family.
Health.
Talent.
Trauma.

They shape the first round of the game. And yet, how we choose to play them—*that's where the real power lies.*

Some people spend years folding because they believe their hand isn't good enough. Others bluff their way through, pretending everything's fine when their soul is begging for change. And then there are those who look at their cards, take a deep breath, and find a way to turn pain into power, and limitation into leadership.

In this life, you don't need a perfect hand to win.
You need self-awareness.
You need emotional clarity.
You need spiritual trust.

Because while you may not control the cards you were given...
you are the only one who can decide how to play them.

Some people are born holding aces—natural charm, privilege,
beauty, or support. They walk into life with confidence, not
because they've earned it, but because their starting hand makes
it easier to believe they'll win.

Others? They get the dreaded 2–7 offsuit—the statistically
worst hand in poker. Life starts harder. They might face neglect,
judgment, scarcity, or pain before they've even had a chance to
play.

But here's the truth poker teaches us:
It's not always the best hand that wins.

It's how you bet.
How you read the moment.
How you trust yourself when others doubt you.
How you don't let one bad hand define the whole game.

You can be born into struggle and still rise.
You can carry wounds and still find healing.
You can grow up unseen and still become a light.

So if you're holding a 2–7, don't fold your story just yet.
Sometimes it's the most unexpected hands that make the most
remarkable comebacks.

But no hand is without potential—depending on how you play
it.

In poker, even the weakest cards can win with the right strategy, timing, and a little faith. The same is true in life. Your beginning doesn't define your becoming.

A painful past can awaken deep empathy.
A disadvantage can spark unmatched determination.
A perceived weakness can become your greatest gift when used with purpose.

Spiritual growth begins when you stop judging your hand and start learning from it. When you begin to ask not *"Why was I dealt this?"* but *"What can I do with it?"*

The truth is, every hand you've ever held has shaped you— taught you, stretched you, and strengthened your soul. Even your worst moments contained the seeds of wisdom.

You don't need to wait for a better deal.
You need to become a better player.

And that starts now.

"In poker, as in life, it's not about the cards you're dealt, but how you play the hand."
— Randy Pausch

✦ Story Vignette – *The Cards You're Dealt*

Jason was born with a congenital heart defect. By the time he turned seven, he'd undergone three surgeries. His classmates never quite knew what to say, so he grew up sitting on the sidelines—watching, observing, rarely chosen for games or birthday parties.

But Jason's mom was a quiet force of nature. Every night, she'd tuck him in with the same words: "You got dealt a tough hand, baby. But I've seen aces win and kings fall. It's how you play."

He didn't fully understand at the time. But by high school, Jason had turned into the most trusted peer mediator in his class—calm, compassionate, and deeply intuitive. He couldn't run marathons. But he could deescalate a hallway fight with one look.

Jason didn't choose his condition. But he *did* choose what he did with it.

REFLECTION PROMPT:
What's in Your Hand?

Take a quiet moment and ask yourself:

- What "cards" were you dealt in life? (Think about your family, upbringing, health, emotional patterns, or early life challenges.)
- Which of those cards have you judged as "bad" or "unfair"?
- How have you *played* those cards so far?
- Is there a hidden strength, lesson, or gift in the hand you were given?
- What would it mean to stop resenting the deal—and start mastering the game?

Write about one card you've been carrying and how it might be calling you to grow.

♠ The Table Takeaway

Poker Wisdom

"Even pocket aces lose 15% of the time."

You can't rely on the strength of your hand alone. Pocket aces may be the best pre-flop combo, but they still get cracked—by bad beats, strange boards, or reckless players who catch luck on the river.

That's the truth about poker: *no guarantees.*
The strongest start can still lead to a loss. The worst hand can sometimes steal the pot.

It's not about control—it's about how you respond. A pro knows when to commit, when to lay it down, and when to trust that the game evens out in the long run.

The lesson? **Respect the odds—but don't worship them.**
Play smart. Stay present. And never confuse a good hand with a guaranteed outcome.

Life Reflection

Life's not much different. Some people are born holding pocket rockets—wealth, beauty, health, support. Others get 7–2 offsuit and have to grind every inch. But the truth? Even the best starting hand can be cracked—and a poor one can win the pot.

CHAPTER 2: The Blind Bets

The Unseen Risks We Take

In poker, every hand starts with what's called the "blinds." These are forced bets—small and big—that players must place before they even see their cards. It's a commitment made in the dark, a willingness to risk something before knowing how the hand will unfold.

And life?
It works the same way.

We take unseen risks all the time—long before we know what the outcome will be. We fall in love, start businesses, speak our truth, or trust someone… without a guarantee. We say yes to paths we can't fully see. We put time, energy, and emotion on the line—*blindly*—because something inside us believes the journey will be worth it.

Sometimes it is. Sometimes it's not. But either way, we grow.

Spiritual growth demands risk. It requires us to step into the unknown, listen to our intuition, and surrender to timing we can't control. We don't get to see the "flop" before we decide to show up. We simply have to trust that even if we're betting blind, there's something bigger guiding the game.

And that kind of trust?
That's how miracles begin.

Some of the biggest bets we ever make are the ones we don't even realize we're making.

As children, we make unconscious agreements based on what we're shown:
"If I stay quiet, I'll be loved."
"If I work hard, I'll be safe."
"If I take care of everyone else, I'll be needed."
"If I shine too brightly, I'll be rejected."

These early choices become the foundation of how we show up in life. We play certain roles, follow certain rules, and suppress certain truths—all because we made blind bets in our earliest hands, with very limited information.

Spiritual trust invites us to examine those old wagers.
To ask: *Did I choose this path, or was I conditioned into it?*
Is this belief really mine, or did I inherit it?
What am I still playing blind at, even now?

Just like poker, we don't always see the full picture when we make our first move. But as life unfolds—card by card, lesson by lesson—we gain clarity. We learn that trust doesn't mean having all the answers. It means being willing to play with heart, even when you can't see the whole hand.

And sometimes, when you're betting on faith alone, you find out that Spirit was never playing *against* you… it was always playing *with* you.

We've all made choices based on partial truths—some that shaped our entire lives.

We took jobs we didn't love because we thought security mattered more than fulfillment.
We stayed in relationships that drained us because we believed love meant sacrifice.
We quieted our intuition to keep the peace, afraid of rocking the boat.

These are the blind bets we make—not out of recklessness, but out of a deep desire to belong, to feel safe, or to survive.

And yet, there comes a time in life—often triggered by loss, disappointment, or awakening—when we begin to see the hand more clearly. The cards on the table start to make sense. We realize we've been playing by someone else's rules, with someone else's fears, and that it's time to rewrite the script.

That's when the real game begins.

Spiritual trust isn't just about having faith in the universe—it's about learning to trust *yourself*. Your inner voice. Your ability to recalibrate, to choose again, and to risk new bets with clearer eyes and an open heart.

Because sometimes the biggest win isn't the pot—it's the *breakthrough*.

When you stop living by old programming…
When you walk away from a game that no longer serves you…
When you take a leap and let the Divine catch you…

That's when the cards shift. That's when the magic happens. Remember: the hand you were dealt doesn't define your destiny. But the courage to play differently—*that just might.*

✦ Story Vignette – *The Blind Bets*

At five years old, Mia decided it was her job to keep her mother happy. She learned quickly that spilled milk meant slammed doors. That laughter could be too loud. That crying earned silence, not comfort.

No one told her to become the peacemaker. She just… did. She learned to read moods like tarot cards, adjusting her tone, her posture, her joy—to keep the energy safe.

By the time she was thirty, Mia was exhausted. Always accommodating. Always agreeable. And completely unsure of what she actually wanted.

One day in therapy, she said aloud for the first time, "I think I made a choice I didn't know I was making." Her voice trembled with the realization.

That was the beginning of everything changing.

REFLECTION PROMPT:
The Blind Bets

What unconscious agreements or beliefs did I make early in life—without fully realizing it?

- Where might I still be playing "blind" based on old survival patterns or inherited expectations?
- What would it look like to trust Spirit more fully in the unknowns of my current life?

Take a few moments to journal freely.
Notice what surfaces without judgment.
Sometimes, just naming the old bet is the first step in changing how you play the next hand.

♠ The Table Takeaway

Poker Wisdom

"You have to post the blinds, whether you like your hand or not."
In every round of poker, someone has to put chips in before seeing their cards. That's the blind. It's not optional—it's the price of staying at the table.

Sometimes, you're forced to act without certainty. You're making a move based on position, rhythm, instinct—not perfect knowledge. You might be betting into the dark, hoping the flop gives you a fighting chance.

It's uncomfortable. Risky. But it's also part of the game.

Great players accept this reality. They don't whine about the blind. They adapt, observe, and learn to play from a disadvantage.

The lesson? **Sometimes life asks for trust before clarity.**
You won't always have all the facts. But you still have to act.

Life Reflection

The "blinds" of life are those moments we commit before we fully understand what's coming: a relationship, a career choice, a leap of faith. Sometimes we have to say yes without a perfect plan.

You don't need certainty to play well.
You need courage, presence... and the willingness to see how the hand unfolds.

CHAPTER 3: Crappy Hands Still Win

Turning Adversity Into Strength

Every poker player knows that you can win a hand with the worst cards on the table—if you know how to play them.
Life, as always, mirrors the game.

We all get dealt painful, messy, or seemingly useless hands at times:
• A diagnosis that alters everything.
• A betrayal you never saw coming.
• A cycle of lack, loss, or loneliness that seems to never end.

But adversity isn't the end of the story. In fact, it's often the *beginning* of your real power.
Just as pressure creates diamonds, adversity has the potential to activate dormant strengths—gifts you wouldn't have found any other way.

Adversity Sharpens Your Intuition

When life doesn't follow the rules, you learn to listen to something deeper.
Pain often awakens the *gut knowing*—the subtle nudges of intuition that no external teacher can give. You begin to sense patterns, energies, and intentions in ways that only those who've walked through fire can understand.

That's not weakness.
That's spiritual discernment born from survival.

Adversity Builds Compassion

People who've experienced true pain tend to be the ones who love the most honestly. Why? Because they *get it.*
They know what it's like to suffer in silence. To rebuild themselves from nothing.
Your struggles become a bridge to others. A medicine only *you* can offer. That's not a handicap—that's a healing gift.

Adversity Creates Courage

Every time you keep going—when you could've quit—you build a deeper reservoir of courage. Not the loud kind, but the sacred kind. The kind that says, *"Even with nothing, I am still here. I am still playing."*
You become a force no one saw coming.

The Spiritual Truth

From a spiritual perspective, adversity is alchemical. It refines you.
You begin to see life not as something happening *to* you, but something awakening *through* you.
The crappy hands you've been dealt are not punishments. They're invitations.
Each one has the potential to show you who you really are, beyond the fear, the conditioning, the self-doubt.

In poker, someone with a bad hand can still win the whole game—if they trust themselves, read the energy of the table, and play with bold, embodied presence.

In life, the same rules apply.

You are not your past.
You are not your pain.
You are not your hand.
You are the *player.*

And once you realize that, you stop waiting for the perfect
deal—and start creating your own wins.

"It's not the cards you're holding—
it's the courage you bring to the
play. A losing hand can still win
when played with heart, timing, and
guts."

Three Real-Life, Symbolic-Style Stories

How a "bad hand" turned into a transformative journey

1. Maya – The Broken Childhood That Became a Healing Gift

Maya grew up in a home filled with addiction, silence, and survival. Her mother disappeared when she was twelve. Her father was emotionally absent. By the time she was a teenager, she had already seen more trauma than most adults.

She used to believe her life was ruined—that she'd been dealt a "bad hand" she'd never recover from. But in her mid-twenties, something shifted. A therapist asked her, "What if you were never broken? What if your sensitivity is your strength?"

That one question led Maya to a path of healing. She began studying trauma-informed care, energy medicine, and inner child work. Eventually, she became a somatic healer, using her lived experience to hold space for others who'd felt abandoned, forgotten, or overwhelmed by life.

Her "bad hand" became a roadmap.
Her pain became her purpose.
And every scar told a story of survival—of spirit outlasting the storm.

2. James – The Bankrupt Entrepreneur Who Learned to Trust Spirit

James was a successful businessman until the 2008 financial crash wiped everything away. He lost his company, his savings, and nearly lost his marriage. For years, he carried shame, believing his failure meant he was worthless.

But with nothing left to lose, James did something he never thought he'd do: he surrendered. He stopped trying to control everything and began listening—really listening—to his inner voice.

That voice led him down a path of spiritual study, self-awareness, and eventually, conscious business coaching. Today, James teaches heart-centered entrepreneurs how to build wealth that aligns with their soul—not just their wallet.

He always says, *"I thought I was losing the game, but Spirit was just reshuffling the deck."*

3. Serena – Chronic Illness and the Power of Inner Wisdom

Serena was diagnosed with a rare autoimmune disease in her early thirties. Doctors gave her pills and predictions. Friends pulled away. She felt isolated, scared, and betrayed by her own body.

But in that deep isolation, she discovered something surprising—*stillness.*
With her career paused, she began meditating. Then journaling. Then exploring energy work and plant medicine. She began to understand her body as more than a vessel—it was a messenger.

Over time, Serena didn't just manage her illness. She transformed her relationship with it. She became a Reiki Master, a medical intuitive, and eventually wrote a book about healing beyond the diagnosis.

Her illness didn't end.
But her suffering did.
And she now says, *"My body was never against me—it was trying to bring me home."*

Each of these stories mirrors the poker table:
The worst hand at first glance...
Turned into the most powerful play—
Because they trusted, transformed, and learned to play with purpose.

Perseverance and Mindset: The Real Game Changers

You've seen the player who loses three hands in a row… and still shows up for the fourth with unwavering presence. You've also seen the one who folds too soon, convinced they can't win—*even when the odds shift in their favor.*

That's not about luck.
That's mindset.
That's perseverance.

In life, as at the poker table, mindset determines everything.
You can't control the deal.
But you can control how you *respond* to it.

You get to choose whether a setback means *"this isn't for me"* or *"this is growing me."*
You get to decide whether discomfort means *"I'm failing"* or *"I'm evolving."*

Here's the truth:
Winning with a bad hand requires two things—belief and endurance.

1. Perseverance: Staying in the Game

Perseverance isn't blind stubbornness. It's sacred resilience.
It's the ability to keep showing up even when life doesn't give you guarantees.
To stay emotionally open even after heartbreak.
To keep taking steps forward even when you can't see the finish line.

Every time you rise again, you gain inner momentum. That movement reshapes your field—spiritually, energetically, and mentally.
It tells the universe, *"I'm not here to quit. I'm here to grow."*

And that's when life starts dealing you differently.

2. Mindset: The Inner Voice That Leads You

Mindset is the story you tell yourself while you're waiting for the next card.
It's how you interpret failure, silence, success, rejection, uncertainty, or delay.

If your inner voice says:

- *"I'm cursed,"* you'll miss opportunities.
- *"This is just how it is,"* you'll stop evolving.
- *"I trust this process,"* you'll find peace in uncertainty.

A powerful mindset doesn't mean you fake confidence.
It means you **return to faith**—again and again—even when fear wants the mic.

And this is where your spiritual work comes in.

Daily rituals, affirmations, grounding practices, journaling, breathwork, Reiki, or prayer—these are all part of your mindset toolkit. They're not luxuries. They're your lifelines when your hand looks hopeless and the pressure is on.

The Long View: The Spiritual Perspective

In poker, you can play a hundred hands and only win a few—but the few that matter can change the entire game.

In life, the same applies. You might fail ten times before
something breaks through.
You may hear a thousand no's before one yes reshapes your
destiny.
But that *one yes...* that *one win...* is often reserved for the ones
who *don't give up.*

Spiritual growth demands you hold faith in the unseen, even
when everything in your environment tells you otherwise.

That's not fantasy.
That's mastery.

✦ Story Vignette – Crappy Hands Still Win

Andre grew up in foster care, passed from home to home like a borrowed book no one finished reading. At sixteen, he'd been expelled twice, arrested once, and told—more than once—that he was going nowhere.

But Andre had a thing for fixing broken electronics. Old radios, discarded laptops, cell phones smashed in frustration—he'd find them, take them apart, and bring them back to life. No one taught him. He just... *knew*.

By twenty-five, he had his own tech repair shop—and a mentorship program for youth who felt just as discarded as the devices they brought in. People asked him how he "turned it around."

He'd just smile and say, "I never had the best cards. I just kept playing."

REFLECTION PROMPT:
Turning Adversity Into Strength

What challenge in my life once felt like a loss—but may have actually reshaped me for the better?

- How did I grow from it emotionally, spiritually, or mentally?
- Am I still resisting any past "bad hands" that might carry hidden wisdom or strength?

Let yourself explore the ways pain has become power. Even the hardest moments can become foundations for something unshakable.

♠ The Table Takeaway

Poker Wisdom

"7–2 offsuit has won championships."
It's the worst starting hand in Texas Hold'em—statistically weak, disconnected, off-suit. No one *wants* to be dealt 7–2. Most fold it immediately.

But here's the twist: sometimes, under the right conditions, with the right read, and the right courage... it *wins.*
Not because the cards were great, but because the player saw an opportunity no one else did—and played it fearlessly.

The board can shift. Opponents can misread you. And when you bet with confidence, you might just take the pot, not by luck—but by daring.

The lesson? **A weak hand doesn't make a weak player.**
Sometimes you don't need better cards—just better play.

Life Reflection

We all get dealt rough hands—loss, trauma, scarcity, setbacks. But none of those define us. How we respond... does.

There are people with every disadvantage who rise to greatness—not because life was fair, but because they refused to fold.

You can play a bad hand well. You can win from behind.
You can make something powerful from something broken.

Keep playing.

Part II:
The Game – How You Play It Matters

Suit: Hearts
Symbolism: Emotions, relationships, intuition, and soul.

CHAPTER 4: Know When to Fold

Letting Go, Walking Away, and Spiritual Surrender

There's a moment in every poker game where the wisest move isn't to stay in—it's to *fold*.

To release the hand.
To accept the loss.
To conserve your energy, your presence, and your peace for another round.

Folding isn't failure.
It's *discernment*.

And in life, that same wisdom is often the most spiritual decision you can make.

Letting Go: The Strength You Don't See Coming

We're conditioned to believe that strength looks like holding on—pushing through, never giving up.
But sometimes, true strength is *knowing when enough is enough.*

Letting go of a toxic relationship.
Letting go of a dream that no longer aligns with your soul.

Letting go of a role you've outgrown.
Letting go of control—of needing to know how it all ends.

Letting go is not giving up.
It's giving *in*—to life's deeper flow, to your higher knowing.

Walking Away: The Sacred Exit

There's a quiet kind of power in walking away with grace.

Not slamming doors.
Not needing validation.
Just *choosing yourself*—your growth, your healing, your peace.

People may not understand.
They may say you're abandoning something good.
But sometimes the soul knows: what looks good isn't what's meant for you anymore.

Walking away is a sacred act.
It says, *"I trust the path ahead more than I fear what I'm leaving behind."*

Spiritual Surrender: When You Stop Forcing and Start Flowing

In poker, staying in a hand you know you can't win is often an emotional decision. Ego, pride, fear of loss—they cloud your judgment and cost you everything.

Life's the same.

When you cling to what no longer fits, you lose far more than time—you lose alignment, energy, and inner clarity.

Spiritual surrender is the opposite of giving up.
It's the radical act of saying:

"I don't have to force what's not flowing. I trust the Divine has a better plan."

It's about aligning your will with a greater intelligence.
It's about being willing to loosen your grip so that what is *meant* for you can arrive.

And here's the most beautiful truth:
Many of your greatest blessings will come *after* you fold the hand you were so afraid to lose.

"You've got to know when to hold 'em, know when to fold 'em."
— Kenny Rogers, *The Gambler*

Not Every Battle Is Yours to Fight

There's a deep spiritual truth we often overlook in the name of strength:
You are not meant to fight every battle that crosses your path.

But the world will try to convince you otherwise.

You'll be told to prove yourself.
To defend your choices.
To argue for your worth.
To "never back down" or "stand your ground"—even when your soul is whispering, *this isn't yours to carry.*

In poker, a wise player doesn't try to win every hand.
They know the energy it takes to battle every deal will burn them out long before the final round.
They fold often—not because they're weak, but because they understand the value of conservation.

Life works the same way.

You're Allowed to Choose Peace Over Proving

Some arguments aren't worth your energy.
Some dynamics are built on unhealed projections you'll never fix.
Some invitations to battle are just distractions dressed as challenges.

Saying *no thank you* doesn't make you passive.
It makes you powerful.

Spiritual maturity means recognizing that you don't need to fight to be right, to be heard, or to be seen.

You don't need to engage just because someone handed you the bait.

You get to ask:

- *Is this fight aligned with my growth?*
- *Will this bring me peace or drain my spirit?*
- *Am I staying out of love… or fear of letting go?*

Release the Warrior Archetype When It No Longer Serves You

Yes, there are times when we must rise and take a stand—when Spirit calls us to act. But not every moment is a battleground. And not every opponent is worth facing.

Sometimes, the greatest act of strength is to step away in stillness, whispering,

"This is not my war."

The world may not applaud that choice.
But your soul will.

And when you protect your energy from unnecessary battles, you reserve your power for the missions that *do* matter. The ones that move you forward. The ones that align with your purpose. The ones that require your full, awakened self.

You are not here to exhaust yourself trying to win every round.
You are here to *evolve.*
And sometimes, evolution means laying the sword down…
And picking your peace instead.

✧ Story Vignette – *Know When to Fold*

Elena spent twelve years in a marriage that looked perfect on the outside. Two kids, nice home, couples' retreats every spring. But behind closed doors, she withered.

The emotional jabs came daily—disguised as jokes. Her voice grew quieter. Her opinions disappeared. Still, she stayed. Because leaving meant failing. And Elena didn't fail.

Then one day, she watched her daughter flinch when her husband raised his voice. That moment split something wide open.

"I'm not leaving for me," she whispered. "I'm folding this hand so she won't grow up thinking *this* is what love is."

She left with nothing but a duffel bag—and finally, her dignity.

REFLECTION PROMPT:
Letting Go, Walking Away, Spiritual Surrender

What have I been holding onto that no longer serves my growth—or my peace?

- Is there something I need to walk away from with grace, not guilt?
- What would spiritual surrender look like in this situation—not giving up, but handing it over?

Reflect gently.
Sometimes the greatest power isn't in holding on—it's in knowing when to release and trust the unseen.

♠ The Table Takeaway

Poker Wisdom

"Good folds save more than good calls."
One of the most disciplined plays in poker isn't a bold bet—it's the quiet decision to let go. You might be holding a decent hand. You might be tempted to chase the turn. But something doesn't feel right.

So you fold. You preserve your stack. You live to play the next hand.

That's not weakness. That's wisdom.

In poker, knowing when to get out is just as important as knowing when to stay in. Chasing losses, feeding ego, or refusing to let go—that's how you go broke.

The lesson? **Don't confuse persistence with purpose.**
Sometimes walking away is the win.

Life Reflection

In life, folding can look like ending a relationship, quitting a draining job, or releasing a dream that no longer fits.

It's hard. It feels like failure. But often, it's freedom.

You're not here to prove something to anyone. You're here to *grow*, to *discern*, to *evolve*.

Letting go isn't giving up. It's creating space for something better to enter.

Fold with grace. Then shuffle up and deal again.

Chapter 5: The Art of the Bluff

Self-Image, Boundaries, and Spiritual Armor

In poker, bluffing isn't about deception—it's about presence.
It's about controlling what others perceive, even when they can't see your hand.
You signal confidence, project calm, and hold your ground...
whether or not the cards support it.

But bluffing in life is more layered. Sometimes it's protective.
Sometimes it's performative.
Sometimes it's survival.

We all wear masks at some point. We project strength when we feel fragile. We say we're fine when we're not. We pretend we have it all together when we're secretly unraveling.
Why? Because *our self-image becomes part of the game.*

Self-Image: Who Are You at the Table?

Your self-image is the way you present yourself to the world—
and the way you *believe* others see you.

It's shaped by early programming, past experiences, and how much you trust your inner voice.
Some people sit at the table of life with a strong hand, but play small because they don't believe they're worthy of winning.

Others play aggressively—not from confidence, but from fear of being seen as weak.

The truth?
The version of you that shows up at the table matters more than the hand you're holding.

Are you leading with truth, or with performance?
Are you playing to win—or playing not to be rejected?

Spiritual growth calls you to align your self-image with your soul-image.
Not who you think you should be.
But who you *are*, beneath the expectations.

Boundaries: Your Personal Table Rules

In poker, every table has rules—what's allowed, what's not. In life, *you* are the one who sets the table for how others interact with you.

Boundaries are how you teach the world to treat you.

Without them, you leak energy.
You overgive, overexplain, overextend—and end up feeling resentful, exhausted, or invisible.

Boundaries are not walls.
They are sacred agreements that say:

- *"This is where I end and you begin."*
- *"This is what's welcome at my table—and what isn't."*
- *"I'm not bluffing when I say I matter."*

A person with clear boundaries doesn't need to bluff to feel powerful.

Their strength is grounded, not performed. Their presence speaks for itself.

Spiritual Armor: Protecting Your Energy Without Losing Your Light

Sometimes, life requires you to bluff a little. To walk into the room with shoulders back and head high—even when you're still healing inside.

That's not being fake.
That's using your **spiritual armor** wisely.

Spiritual armor isn't about pretending.
It's about energetic protection—choosing where to shine, where to share, and where to hold sacred space for yourself.

Your armor might be:

- A mantra before walking into a difficult space.
- A visualization of light surrounding you.
- A silent affirmation that says, *"I am rooted, I am clear, I am enough."*
- A refusal to explain your worth to those unwilling to see it.

Armor is temporary. It helps you stay grounded until your full authenticity feels safe again.

The Real Art of the Bluff

In poker, bluffing is about protecting your strategy.

In life, the "bluff" becomes a metaphor for managing perception while staying anchored in truth.

You don't need to lie about who you are.
You don't need to fake joy, or confidence, or alignment.
But you *do* need to protect your energy, your vision, your
becoming.

Your greatest power isn't in what people see.
It's in who you know yourself to be—even when no one else is
looking.

That's not a bluff.
That's sovereignty.

Projecting Confidence in Uncertainty

There comes a moment in every game—poker or life—where you don't know what's coming next.
The turn hasn't revealed itself.
The stakes feel high.
You're holding your breath, holding your hand, and trying to decide what to do.

In those moments, projecting confidence isn't about arrogance or pretending.
It's about choosing to anchor in **presence** when you don't have control over the outcome.

This isn't about bluffing in a manipulative way.
It's about embodying inner steadiness when the outer world is full of unknowns.

Uncertainty Is the Portal to Growth

Growth always comes with a side of doubt.
When you're on the edge of change, your ego panics. Your fear voice gets loud.
"What if I fail?"
"What if I'm not enough?"
"What if this was a mistake?"

But spiritual confidence isn't the absence of fear.
It's the **willingness to keep showing up** anyway.
To say, *"Even though I can't see the next card, I trust myself to meet it."*

Energy Leads Before Evidence

Here's a powerful truth most people overlook:
People respond not to your certainty, but to your *energy*.

If you project groundedness, openness, quiet power…
You shift the atmosphere—even if you're not sure what's next.
You create space for trust, clarity, and synchronicity to emerge.

This is especially important when:

- You're walking into a new opportunity that scares you.
- You're stepping into leadership for the first time.
- You're making a choice that no one else understands.
- You're healing from something the world says should've broken you.

In those moments, you don't need to fake it.

But you *do* need to root yourself in intention and act as if the next card is already aligned in your favor.

Confidence in uncertainty is not pretending to know.
It's trusting that you'll rise to meet whatever comes.

Spiritual Practice for Embodying Quiet Confidence

Try this before entering a high-stakes or emotionally charged situation:

1. Close your eyes. Feel your feet on the ground.
2. Breathe into your belly. Imagine a warm light filling your core.

3. Repeat silently:
   "I don't need to know the outcome. I trust who I am becoming."
4. Open your eyes, lift your chin slightly, and walk in with grace.

You don't have to be loud to be powerful.
You don't have to be certain to be steady.
You just have to show up as the version of you who trusts the deeper unfolding.

Because often, the energy you project becomes the energy that calls in your next win.

✦ Story Vignette – The Art of the Bluff

Devon stood backstage, palms sweating, heart racing. He was minutes away from pitching his startup to a room full of investors. What they didn't know? He hadn't slept in two nights. His bank account was almost empty. And he had no backup plan.

But he adjusted his blazer, squared his shoulders, and walked onto that stage with the calm confidence of a man who had nothing to lose—and everything to prove.

He spoke like a seasoned pro. Made them laugh. Showed them his vision. And when he walked off to a standing ovation, he realized: he wasn't bluffing anymore.

He *was* that guy now.

REFLECTION PROMPT:
The Art of the Bluff

When have I had to project confidence even when I didn't feel it inside?

- What did that moment teach me about resilience, energy, or presence?
- How can I create a deeper alignment between how I show up outwardly and how I feel inwardly?

Explore how you hold your energy.
Sometimes the "bluff" isn't deception—it's practicing the posture of the person you're becoming.

♠ The Table Takeaway

Poker Wisdom

"The bluff isn't about deception—it's about reading the moment."
Bluffing isn't lying. It's storytelling under pressure. It's knowing how to project strength when your hand is weak—and sensing when your opponent is more afraid than you are.

A bluff can win the pot without ever needing the cards.
But it's not random—it's strategic. The best bluffs come from confidence, timing, and understanding human behavior.

Too many bluffs? You lose trust.
No bluffs at all? You become predictable.

The lesson? **A bluff is a mirror—it reflects what others expect to see.**
And sometimes, projecting power helps you reclaim it.

Life Reflection

In life, we all bluff a little—on stage, at work, in moments of vulnerability. We stand tall when we're shaking. We smile when we're unsure.

That's not fake—*it's courage in action.*

Sometimes the bluff is survival. Sometimes it's strategy.
Either way, it's part of learning when to show your truth—and when to hold it close.

Your energy speaks louder than your words. So make it count.

Chapter 6: Gut Instinct is Your Guide

The Power of Intuition

In poker, intuition can change the game.
A glance, a hesitation, a flicker of energy across the table—and something inside you *knows.*
You can't explain it.
You can't prove it.
But the signal is clear: *"Something's off... or something's right."*

In life, intuition works the same way.

It's the quiet voice beneath the noise.
The soft nudge before the mind catches up.
The subtle shift in your body that says, *"Pay attention."*

And the more you listen, the louder it becomes.

Intuition Is a Soul Skill

Intuition isn't a luxury for the "spiritually gifted."
It's your birthright.

You were born with the ability to sense energy, truth, timing, and alignment.

You've likely used it more times than you realize:

- Walking away from someone who seemed "nice" but didn't feel safe.
- Accepting an opportunity that didn't make logical sense—but changed your life.
- Saying no when everything in your body screamed *yes to yourself.*
- Trusting a dream, vision, or knowing you couldn't explain.

That was your intuition.
That was your gut at the table, whispering, *"You're not alone in this."*

Why We Ignore It

The world teaches us to prioritize logic, reason, and external validation.
We're rewarded for being rational, not intuitive.
We're told to "prove it," not to *feel it.*

So we silence the part of us that *knows.*
We override the instinct.
We betray the gut feeling.
And later, we say things like:

- *"I knew something was wrong."*
- *"I should've listened to myself."*
- *"I felt it in my bones, but I didn't trust it."*

Ignoring your intuition is like folding the winning hand because someone told you it wasn't worth playing.

Tuning In: Your Internal Guidance System

Intuition speaks in different ways for different people:

- A tingling in your body.
- A wave of peace or discomfort.
- A mental image.
- A strong sense of "yes" or "no" with no obvious logic.
- A message in a dream.
- A synchronistic sign or repeated symbol.

It's not always loud—but it is consistent.

And when you begin to honor it, you strengthen the channel. You begin to move through life more fluidly, more intentionally, more aligned with the unfolding path.

The Spiritual Role of Intuition

Your intuition is your direct line to Spirit.
It's how your soul guides you through the fog.
It won't always lead you to what's easy—but it will always lead you to what's true.

In the game of life, intuition is your inner compass.
It's how you navigate uncertainty without losing yourself.
It's how you read the table when the cards don't make sense.

When you trust it, even when others don't understand, you claim your power.
You begin to live in flow, not force.
In alignment, not approval.

And that's how you begin to win—not just at the table… but in every part of your life.

Listen to Your Gut: The Sacred Signals You Can't Ignore

Intuition doesn't just speak in feelings.
Sometimes it *shouts* through synchronicities.
Sometimes it *whispers* through dreams.
Sometimes it *shows up* as a deep, wordless knowing that bypasses logic entirely.

And when you begin to live attuned to these signs, life starts to feel different.
More fluid. More aligned. More guided.

Synchronicities: Divine Nudges in Disguise

You think of someone, and they call.
You ask a question, and a book falls off the shelf with the exact answer.
You see repeating numbers, signs, symbols—again and again— and something inside you *knows* it's not random.

These are synchronicities—spiritual breadcrumbs pointing you toward your next step.

In poker, synchronicities might look like a "lucky streak" or the right card flipping at the perfect moment. But those "coincidences" are often the result of being in energetic alignment—when your inner world and outer world are in sync.

When you're grounded, clear, and open, you create a field where these nudges can land.
They're not just happening around you…
They're happening *for* you.

Dreams: Your Soul's Language

Dreams are your subconscious—or your soul—processing what your waking mind is too busy to grasp.
Sometimes dreams feel symbolic, mystical, even prophetic.
Other times they're messy, fragmented, or repetitive.

But dreams can carry messages if you're willing to listen.

A recurring image.
A feeling that lingers long after waking.
A dream that seems too "real" to ignore.

These moments are worth noting. Worth journaling. Worth meditating on.

Dreams are like receiving a hand you didn't expect—but that holds more potential than you realize.

Inner Knowing: The Truth Beneath the Noise

And then there's the most subtle yet profound form of guidance: inner knowing.

Not a thought.
Not a feeling.
But a certainty that doesn't need explanation.

You might feel it in your gut, in your chest, or deep in your nervous system.
It's calm, not anxious. Quiet, not loud.
And when it speaks, you feel aligned.

This is the voice of your higher self.
Your deepest intelligence.
Your divine wisdom.

What Happens When You Actually Listen

When you begin to honor these signals—gut feelings, dreams, synchronicities—you change how you play the game of life.

You stop asking for proof.
You start acting on trust.
You move when guided—not when pressured.

And with time, you stop needing to bluff.
Because you've learned to move with something much more powerful than appearances:
inner truth.

The game changes when you stop looking at the cards and start listening to your soul.

✦ Story Vignette – Gut Instinct is Your Guide

Sariah had already signed the contract. The new clinic was sleek, well-funded, and promised more than double her current income. Her friends toasted to her success. Her mentor said it was the obvious next step.

But something inside her buzzed. Not anxiety—something deeper. A subtle *no* that pulsed just beneath her ribs.

Three days before her start date, she pulled out. No explanation. Just trust.

Six months later, headlines broke: the clinic was under investigation for insurance fraud.

Sariah didn't say "I told you so."
She just lit a candle, closed her eyes, and whispered, "Thank you."

REFLECTION PROMPT:
Gut Instinct Is Your Guide

When was a time I trusted my gut—and it turned out to be right?

- How did that knowing feel in my body?
- Where in my life am I currently being nudged by intuition, even if I can't explain it logically?

Take time to tune in.
Your gut doesn't need to make sense to others—only to *you*.

♠ The Table Takeaway

Poker Wisdom

"When logic and instinct clash—listen to your gut."
Poker is more than math. You can know the odds, track the betting, and still feel something off—the kind of quiet nudge no stat sheet can explain.

That's your intuition. And elite players trust it.

Maybe it's the way someone tossed their chips. Maybe it's the silence.
You don't *know*—but you *know.*

The gut doesn't shout. It whispers. And when you listen, it often saves you.

The lesson? **Instinct is a trained muscle—use it.**
Data is helpful. Patterns are powerful. But sometimes, the gut call is the only one that wins.

Life Reflection

Life won't always make sense on paper.
Sometimes you'll feel pulled toward something with no logic to back it up—just a deep knowing in your body.

Trust it.
Your intuition is your soul's compass. It's the quiet wisdom that sees what your eyes can't.

The best decisions aren't always the safest—they're the *truest.*

So when the inner voice speaks... don't fold.

Chapter 7: Table Talk and Energy Reads

Reading Others, Energy Fields, and Spiritual Discernment

In poker, the best players don't just watch the cards—they watch the people.

They study the energy at the table.
The microexpressions.
The posture shifts.
The tone behind the table talk.

They don't always win because they hold better cards.
They win because they can read the field.

And in life, especially on a spiritual path, the same skill becomes vital—spiritual discernment.

Reading Energy Is a Survival Skill—and a Superpower

From a young age, many sensitive souls learn to read the room without even realizing it.
They pick up tension before it's spoken.
They sense when someone's words don't match their energy.
They feel unsafe before there's any logical reason.

That's not paranoia.
That's perception.

You are an energetic being, walking through a world full of invisible information.

Reading energy isn't just about protecting yourself from toxicity.
It's about moving through life more intelligently—choosing aligned relationships, right timing, and grounded decisions based on *what's real*, not just what's presented.

How Energy Reading Works

Everyone emits an energy field—a vibrational signature made up of their thoughts, emotions, beliefs, and intentions.
Some people shine with clarity and calm.
Others carry storm clouds of stress, resentment, or unspoken pain.

You may not "see" it… but you *feel* it.

You know when someone enters a room and lifts it.
You know when someone walks past you and your body tenses.

That's energetic awareness.

In poker, this is called "table presence."
In life, it's intuition meets discernment.

Spiritual Discernment: Seeing What's True Beneath What's Shown

Discernment isn't judgment.
It's clarity.

It's your ability to tell the difference between:

- Who someone is vs. who they pretend to be
- An aligned opportunity vs. a shiny distraction
- Real connection vs. energetic hooks or projections

Spiritual discernment comes from inner stillness—not suspicion.
The more grounded you are, the more clearly you feel what's yours and what isn't.

This is how you stop leaking energy to people-pleasing, overexplaining, and second-guessing.

Protecting Your Energy at the Table of Life

Just as poker players guard their tells, you also must protect your energy.

That means:

- Shielding your aura before entering crowded or emotionally charged spaces
- Tuning in before trusting—even if someone's words sound right
- Withdrawing your energy from people who drain, manipulate, or confuse you
- Listening to your body—it always knows when something's off

Energetic hygiene isn't mystical fluff.
It's a daily practice of sovereignty.

Trust What You Feel, Even If You Can't Yet Explain It

You may not always be able to "prove" what you feel...
But your soul will always know.

Over time, the more you honor that knowing, the less you
tolerate misalignment.
You'll feel repelled by falsehood and drawn to truth.
You'll stop playing small at tables where you don't belong.
You'll sit where energy flows, not where it's forced.

Because when you can read the room with spiritual eyes, you
stop needing permission.
You just know.
And that knowing?
That's your edge.

Discernment is the quiet superpower of those who walk with
Spirit.
You don't have to call it out. You just have to feel it—and
move accordingly.

Empaths, Energy Healers, and Intuitives: The Sensitive Players at the Table

Empaths. Intuitives. Energy healers.
You're not just playing the game—you *feel* the game. Deeply. Sometimes painfully.
You don't just see people's expressions—you feel their emotions ripple through your nervous system like a wave.
You sense energy shifts before anyone speaks.
You walk into a room and can tell who's carrying joy… and who's barely holding it together.

This isn't imagination.
It's **energetic sensitivity**.
And while it can feel like a burden, it's actually a form of *spiritual intelligence.*

The Empath's Experience: Absorbing the Atmosphere

Empaths often struggle not because they're weak—but because they haven't been taught how to manage what they feel.

You:

- Absorb moods and unspoken emotions
- Feel tired after being around others
- Need extra alone time to recharge
- Struggle with boundaries, because you feel others' needs so acutely

In poker terms, you're the one at the table feeling everyone else's pressure—even when the hand isn't yours.
You read the tension.
You *know* when someone's bluffing, even if you say nothing.

But without tools, empathy becomes energetic overload.
And that's why discernment and energetic boundaries are critical.

Energy Healers: Transmuters of Frequency

If you're an energy healer—Reiki practitioner, bodyworker, intuitive guide—you don't just feel energy…
You work with it.

Your hands, your voice, your presence—they carry vibration.
And you're often drawn to people in pain, chaos, or transition because your soul remembers how to hold space for healing.

But here's the challenge:
Many energy healers give away their power.
They over-extend. They "fix." They pour out until they're empty.

You can't heal sustainably without energetic protection, regular clearing, and a deep trust that you're a channel—not the source.

At the table of life, the healer's work is subtle but profound.
You don't need to control the outcome—you just need to keep your field clean and your presence strong.

Intuitives: Translators of the Unseen

Intuitives receive downloads, visions, knowings, and energetic cues that others might miss.
You're the one who gets "a feeling" and ends up being right.
You know who to trust—without being told.
You sense timing. Truth. Flow.

But in a world that values proof, intuitives often doubt themselves.

The key to developing intuitive power is **trusting without needing validation.**
You don't need approval to be aligned.
You don't need credentials to carry wisdom.

Intuition is your birthright.
And the more you honor it, the stronger it becomes.

The Common Thread: Sensitivity Is Strength

Whether you identify as an empath, a healer, an intuitive—or all three—you are not weak.
You are not too much.
You are not imagining things.

You are wired to feel more.
And that feeling, when refined and supported, becomes your **superpower.**

It helps you navigate the table with grace.
It helps you know who's real and who's pretending.
It helps you fold the right hands, and go all-in when it matters.

You don't need to play louder.
You just need to play clearer—aligned with your energy, guided by your truth, and rooted in your own sacred frequency.

✦ Story Vignette – *Table Talk and Energy Reads*

Marc had always been good with people. But it wasn't what they *said* that he listened to—it was everything underneath. The hesitation in their laugh. The way their eyes darted just before a big claim. The shift in posture when they felt exposed.

At networking events, he rarely spoke first. He just *watched*. Felt. Noticed.

One night, at a poker table in Vegas, a man across from him smiled too wide when placing a large bet. His hands were still. But Marc felt a ripple of tension rise off him like heat.

Marc called.
The man was bluffing.

The dealer pushed the chips toward Marc, but he barely noticed. He was too busy smiling at the confirmation: energy never lies.

REFLECTION PROMPT:
Table Talk and Energy Reads

What do I tend to sense or feel around certain people—beyond what they say?

- Can I recall a time I picked up on someone's true energy before the facts were clear?
- How can I better honor what I *feel*, even if it contradicts appearances?

Energy doesn't lie.
Use your intuition like a compass—and trust your inner read more than the surface game.

♠ The Table Takeaway

Poker Wisdom

"The real game isn't on the table—it's in the players."
Watch the hands. Listen to the talk. Feel the tension shift when someone bets big or stays quiet. That's table presence—and it's just as telling as the cards.

Poker is a game of energy reads.
Is that laugh forced? Is their silence calculated—or scared?
The words matter less than the vibe behind them.

Great players don't just play the hand—they play the room.

The lesson? **Every action sends a signal. Learn to read the pulse beneath the play.**

If you can feel what's not being said, you'll always have an edge.

Life Reflection

People carry energy, just like players carry tells.
You know when something feels off—even if no one says a word.

Learning to read that energy is a superpower.
Whether in a boardroom, a breakup, or a spiritual shift... your ability to feel the undercurrent helps you respond with wisdom, not just reaction.

Listen with more than your ears.
Feel what's underneath.
Trust the read—and play accordingly.

Chapter 8: Playing the Long Game

Patience, Personal Evolution, and Karmic Cycles

In poker, the best players know that one hand doesn't define the game.

You can lose ten rounds in a row…
and still win the night.
You can hold back, observe, wait, and make one well-timed move—
and shift everything.

That's the art of the long game.
And in life, this wisdom is even more profound.

The most meaningful growth doesn't come from instant wins.
It comes from slow shifts. Quiet awakenings. Seasons of waiting, learning, and unlearning.

Patience: Trusting the Timing You Can't Control

Spiritual patience isn't passive.
It's presence without pressure.
It's the ability to *stay at the table* even when nothing is going your way.

The truth is, some of the most important hands in your life—relationships, purpose, abundance, healing—aren't meant to arrive quickly.
They're meant to *arrive right.*

If you rush the game, you miss the deeper pattern.
You force what was meant to flow.
You accept less than what Spirit intended for you, just because you got tired of waiting.

Patience doesn't mean you sit back and do nothing.
It means you stay in alignment while life reshuffles.
It means you learn to feel safe in the *in-between.*

Personal Evolution: Growth Doesn't Always Look Like Winning

We love the visible wins—promotions, breakthroughs, big transformations.
But true personal evolution often happens underground.
In silence.
In setbacks.
In the choices no one sees but your soul.

You evolve when:

- You stop reacting and start responding.
- You speak up when silence once ruled you.
- You walk away from what once kept you trapped.
- You forgive, even when the apology never came.
- You trust yourself, even when the outcome is uncertain.

In poker, a great player evolves by watching others, learning from losses, and adjusting their strategy.
In life, *you* evolve by becoming more aware, more intuitive, more soul-led.

The person you were five years ago may have folded.
The person you're becoming?
Knows exactly when to hold, when to wait, and when to walk away.

That's personal mastery.
And it's never instant.
It's earned.

Karmic Cycles: Playing Out the Unfinished Patterns

Karma isn't punishment—it's momentum.
It's the patterns you carry, the stories you repeat, the energy you return to again and again... until you choose differently.

Have you ever noticed that life brings you the same kind of person, problem, or situation—again and again—until you finally *change your response*?

That's a karmic cycle.
You're not stuck—you're *looping* through the same lesson... until your soul integrates it.

In poker, a player who never learns from their patterns loses over and over.
In life, the same applies.

But once you see the pattern, you hold power.

You break the cycle when you:

- Choose worth over scarcity
- Trust your intuition over external noise
- Set a boundary instead of betraying yourself
- Stop chasing what doesn't value you

You complete the karmic round not by winning—but by *waking up*.

Why the Long Game Is Worth It

Patience, evolution, and karmic wisdom don't bring quick satisfaction.
But they bring *lasting transformation.*

They don't win you the flashy hands.
But they win you the kind of life that's built on soul integrity, not illusion.

You are not here to be quick.
You're here to be *true.*

And in the long game, that's what ultimately wins.

The soul always plays the long game.
It doesn't rush the lesson.
It reshuffles the deck until you remember who you really are.

Some Wins Take Years to Come Around

There's a moment in every long game—whether it's poker, business, healing, or love—when you wonder if it's even worth staying in.

You've played your hand with integrity.
You've done the inner work.
You've followed your intuition, said your prayers, visualized, journaled, surrendered...

And still—nothing.
Or worse, losses.

This is where most people fold.
Not because they've lost—but because they've grown tired of *waiting to win.*

But here's the thing:
Some wins are slow because they're sacred.
Because they require things to align beyond just your own timeline.
Because they're not just about you—they're about divine timing, unseen connections, karmic closure, and soul readiness.

Delayed Doesn't Mean Denied

In poker, some players sit through dozens of quiet hands, slow rounds, and endless waiting before the cards finally fall in their favor.
But when that winning hand arrives—it changes the entire game.

In life, some of your greatest blessings will come *after* the part where you wanted to give up.
They'll arrive when you've matured into the version of you

that's ready to receive them.
Not from desperation.
Not from proving.
But from alignment.

A soulmate doesn't arrive while you're still clinging to what's
safe.
Your real purpose doesn't appear while you're stuck in
performance.
True abundance doesn't stay when you're playing small.

These wins require you to *become* someone new.
And that takes time.

Everything You've Lived Is Preparing You

The job you didn't get?
It taught you how to trust your value.

The relationship that broke you open?
It revealed your patterns—and your resilience.

The season of waiting, wandering, wondering?
It built your patience, your voice, your inner knowing.

Nothing is wasted.
It may not make sense yet, but life remembers what you've
invested in faith, effort, and self-discovery.
And when the moment comes, it will feel like *everything you
went through was building toward that one breakthrough.*

Because it was.

Trust the Arc

The timeline of your soul is longer and wiser than the timeline of your ego.
It's not in a hurry.
It's here for *depth*, not drama.

And the game of life isn't about winning quickly.
It's about playing *faithfully*—especially when it looks like nothing is happening.

Your win may be one hand away.
One conversation.
One inspired moment of alignment.
One inner shift that flips everything.

So don't quit on the game.
Don't walk away from the table just before it turns.

Some wins take years to come around—because they're worth the wait.
Because they change everything.
Because they were never just about winning…
They were about ***becoming.***

✦ Story Vignette – Playing the Long Game

At 22, Aisha pitched her holistic wellness program to five clinics. Rejected.
At 26, she tried again—more polished, more confident. Still, no one bit.
At 31, she almost quit altogether, wondering if her dream was just too niche. Too early. Too… hers.

But instead of quitting, she built her own tiny online platform. Posted consistently. Shared what she knew. Taught one client at a time.

By 37, her videos had gone viral, her course had 10,000 students, and one of the same clinics that had once turned her away was now asking *her* to consult.

She never won fast. She won slow—and *on purpose.*

REFLECTION PROMPT:
Playing the Long Game

Where in my life am I being asked to be patient, even when results aren't immediate?

- What soul lesson might be unfolding beneath the delays?
- How can I shift from frustration to trust in the bigger picture?

Not all wins happen in the first few rounds.
Sometimes the deepest growth happens while you're waiting for the right card to turn.

♠ The Table Takeaway

Poker Wisdom

"One hand doesn't define your night."
You can lose a big pot and still win the session. The best players don't chase every win—they manage their stack, their mindset, and their stamina.

Poker is about endurance, not ego.
You'll face bad beats, boring stretches, and players who try to tilt you off balance. But if you're in it for the long game, you don't panic. You play with perspective.

The lesson? **Patience pays. Tilt costs. Stay in rhythm, not reaction.**

If you keep playing smart, your edge will show up.

Life Reflection

Life isn't about instant wins.
Some seasons feel slow. Some paths are winding. But progress is still progress—even if it's not flashy.

This chapter reminds you to zoom out.
You're building something bigger than this moment. A single setback doesn't cancel your journey. A bad day doesn't erase your worth.

Play the long game.
Trust the process.
And know that staying in alignment is always more powerful than rushing for results.

Part III:
The Turn – When
Life Gets Wild

Suit: Clubs
Symbolism: Action, growth,
willpower, and spiritual work.

Chapter 9: When the Turn Surprises You

Unexpected Events: Health, Betrayal, and Miracles

In *Texas Hold'em* poker, the "turn" is the fourth card placed face up on the table.
It changes everything.

You could be winning, and suddenly the turn takes it all away.
You could be losing, and the turn brings in the card you never expected.

It's the moment in the game where what seemed certain becomes uncertain—
And what was once hopeless gains new life.

In life, the turn comes just as unpredictably.

A diagnosis.
A betrayal.
A job offer that changes your direction.
A chance encounter that rewrites your timeline.
A miracle you never saw coming.

You didn't plan for it.
You couldn't have predicted it.

But now it's on the table—and you have to decide how to play the rest of the hand.

Health: When Your Body Becomes the Messenger

Nothing brings you face-to-face with your mortality, your truth, or your priorities like a health crisis.
Whether it's your own body or someone you love, illness is one of life's harshest turns.

It slows you down.
It forces you inward.
It strips away everything superficial and asks, *"What really matters now?"*

Some people see illness as punishment.
But often, it's a call to recalibrate.
To heal—not just the body, but the life that surrounds it.

Health issues don't just interrupt your plans.
They often *reveal* what wasn't sustainable in the first place.

They call you into presence.
Into surrender.
Into a deeper kind of faith.

Betrayal: The Sharp Turn of the Soul

Few things hit harder than betrayal.
When someone you trusted flips their hand and it's nothing like what you believed—
It breaks something open.

Betrayal is a sacred turn in the game of life.
It cuts deep, not just because of the loss, but because of what it forces you to see.

It shows you:

- Where you ignored your intuition
- Where you gave too much without reciprocity
- Where you believed in potential instead of reality

But betrayal also brings power—if you let it.

It teaches discernment.
It clarifies boundaries.
It returns you to your own knowing.

It may break your heart...
But it also breaks the illusion you were living in.

And that, too, is a gift.

Miracles: The Turn You Didn't Dare Ask For

Then there are the turns that bless you beyond logic.
A prayer answered.
A healing that defies medical explanation.
A phone call that changes your future.
A breakthrough that comes in the final hour—just as you were about to give up.

These are the miracle turns.
They arrive without warning, and they remind you:

The game isn't rigged against you.
The Divine is always playing a longer hand.

Sometimes, you're being protected.
Sometimes, you're being positioned.
Sometimes, you're being prepared for more than you imagined possible.

And sometimes, just when you think it's over…
Life turns the card that brings it all together.

How Will You Respond to the Turn?

Whether it comes as pain or blessing, the turn always asks
something of you.

Will you react… or respond?
Collapse… or rise?
Cling to the old hand… or adapt to the new one?

You don't get to choose the card.
But you *do* get to choose the meaning you make from it—
And the energy you bring to what comes next.

Because the turn isn't the end of the game.
It's the *pivot point.*
The space between breakdown and breakthrough.
The test before the transformation.

And if you stay present—stay wise—stay open…
You'll find that even the most painful turns can lead to your
highest alignment.

Staying Grounded When Everything Shifts

The turn card doesn't ask for your permission.
It arrives when it arrives—fast, unexpected, and often unsettling.
And when it hits—whether through crisis, betrayal, awakening, or blessing—your nervous system goes into high alert.
Your thoughts scramble.
Your emotions spike.
Your plans crumble.

And yet…
this is the moment you're being asked to root.

To return to center.
To breathe, feel, and *remember who you are*—even when the landscape around you is shifting beneath your feet.

Because how you respond to change often determines whether it becomes a breakdown or a breakthrough.

The Importance of Spiritual Anchors

Staying grounded doesn't mean pretending everything is okay.
It means creating inner stillness in the middle of external chaos.

It means leaning on the tools that tether you to your soul:

- Deep, conscious breathing
- Journaling what's real—not what's pretty
- Walking in nature to reconnect with Earth's rhythm
- Energy clearing to reset your field
- Praying, meditating, or placing your hand over your heart and whispering, *"I am safe in myself."*

These are not indulgences.
They are lifelines.
Because when the ground shakes, your nervous system needs
ritual, rhythm, and reconnection to stay steady.

The World May Shift—But You Don't Have To Collapse With It

The truth is, everything can change in an instant:

- A phone call
- A diagnosis
- A revelation
- A sudden ending… or beginning

And when that moment comes, the part of you that wants to
control will panic.
The part of you that wants to *understand* will spin.
The part of you that wants to *fix* will reach for anything to
stabilize.

But the wise part of you—the soul part—knows:

*"I don't need to fix this. I need to feel this. I need to stay with
myself in this."*

That's grounding.
That's maturity.
That's spiritual leadership from the inside out.

Grounding Is Power Without Force

In poker, the grounded player is the most dangerous one at the
table.
Not because they bluff big—but because they don't waver.
They watch. They breathe. They feel the energy.
They wait for the right moment to act.

In life, grounding gives you the same advantage.

When you stay rooted during emotional upheaval, you become a clear vessel.
You hear your intuition more clearly.
You respond with wisdom instead of reactivity.
You allow the shift to shape you—not shatter you.

Staying grounded when everything shifts doesn't stop the storm.
But it ensures you're not swept away by it.

When the turn comes—
Root deeper.
Move slower.
Breathe longer.
And trust that even in the chaos…
you are being re-aligned with something greater.

✧ Story Vignette – When the Turn Surprises You

Caleb had it all lined up—tenure track teaching job, engagement ring in his sock drawer, mortgage pre-approved. Life felt predictable, secure, solid.

Then, the turn card hit: his fiancée ended things out of nowhere. Said she couldn't pretend anymore.
That same week, the university cut funding for his department.

At first, Caleb unraveled. Everything he'd built seemed to dissolve in one swoop. But with nothing to lose, he said yes to something he'd always denied himself: a year abroad. Teaching English in Bali, writing poetry again, sleeping under stars instead of deadlines.

What looked like collapse… was actually redirection.

The turn didn't betray him.
It freed him.

REFLECTION PROMPT:
When the Turn Surprises You

What unexpected event in my life changed everything—
whether for better or worse?

- How did I respond in that moment, and what did it teach
  me about myself?
- Where might I still be resisting change instead of
  exploring what it could reveal?

Sometimes what feels like disruption is really divine
redirection.
Look again—there may be deeper wisdom in the chaos.

♠ The Table Takeaway

Poker Wisdom

"The turn changes everything."
You go into the flop with a plan—then the turn card hits, and suddenly, the odds shift. A flush draw completes. A pair becomes a full house. Or what felt strong now looks fragile.

The turn doesn't care about your expectations. It just *is.*

Great players adapt instantly. They re-evaluate, release attachment, and play what's real—not what they *wish* it were.

The lesson? **You can't fight the turn. But you can decide how you respond to it.**

Resilience isn't about controlling the cards—it's about recalibrating when they surprise you.

Life Reflection

Life delivers "turn cards" all the time—unexpected diagnoses, losses, miracles, betrayals, offers, endings.

It doesn't mean you did something wrong. It just means the game shifted.

This chapter asks: Can you stay centered when the plan changes? Can you pivot without panic? Can you trust that sometimes, the turn that breaks your hand is redirecting your soul?

When life surprises you, don't fold in fear.
Pause. Breathe. Reassess.
And remember: one more card is still coming.

Chapter 10: The River Card – Game Changer or Heartbreaker

The Final Piece Falling into Place... or Falling Apart

In poker, the river is the final card.
After all the anticipation, risk, intuition, and calculation—
One last card hits the table.
And it either completes the hand...
Or destroys it.

It's the moment everything becomes clear.
The win.
The loss.
The truth.

And in life, the river shows up just the same.
Not always when you want it—
But always when it's time.

When Everything Falls Into Place

Sometimes the river card feels like divine alignment.
You get the call.
The opportunity appears.
The clarity you've been craving finally lands in your heart like a soft, certain yes.

In those moments, it all makes sense.

You see why the past didn't work.
You understand the timing.
You realize you weren't being delayed—you were being prepared.

The wait was building your readiness.
The uncertainty was fine-tuning your faith.
The silence was deepening your intuition.

And now, here it is:
The last card.
And it completes the hand in ways you couldn't have scripted.

These moments feel like grace.
Like your soul whispering, *"Told you it was coming. Trust was never wasted."*

When Everything Falls Apart

But not every river is a miracle.
Some river cards arrive and leave you breathless in the worst way.

The truth comes out.
The person leaves.
The deal falls through.
The diagnosis is final.
The loss becomes real.

You thought the final card would save you.
Instead, it breaks you.

These moments feel brutal.
Empty.
Unfair.

You question everything—your path, your worth, even your intuition.
And it's okay.
You're human.
You're allowed to grieve the ending you didn't want.

But here's the deeper truth:
Even when the river breaks your heart, it brings you clarity.

It shows you what is no longer sustainable.
What was built on illusion.
What was ready to end.
What was never meant to stay.

It may feel like the game is over.
But in reality—

it's a sacred reset.

The collapse creates space for what's real.
And that, too, is grace.

The Gift of the River: Truth

Whether the river completes your hand or leaves you empty…
It *always* reveals truth.

And spiritual maturity means being able to hold both kinds of rivers:

- The ones that deliver joy
- And the ones that initiate you through loss

Because either way, you're being shaped.
Either way, something sacred is unfolding.
Either way, you are being led closer to your soul's next becoming.

The river card isn't the end—it's the reveal.
And no matter what shows up…
You are still in the game.

Faith in Divine Timing

The river card always comes *after* the waiting.
After the bets.
After the unknowns.
After the tension of not knowing whether to hold on or let go.

And just like life, it arrives *on its own schedule.*
Not when you want it.
Not when you think you're ready.
But when your soul *actually* is.

This is where faith in divine timing becomes everything.

When You've Done the Work, but Nothing's Happening

There are seasons when you're all in:

- Doing the inner work
- Healing the old wounds
- Saying the affirmations
- Honoring your path
- Listening to your intuition

And still—silence.
No big break.
No breakthrough.
Just… stillness.

It's tempting to believe the river won't come.
That maybe you missed your shot.
That maybe all your effort was wasted.

But in spiritual truth, delays are not denials.
They are *refinements.*

Divine timing often holds back the final card until:

- Your nervous system can hold the blessing
- Your heart is no longer operating from lack
- You've stopped trying to *force* alignment and instead surrendered to flow

The universe doesn't operate on your clock.
It operates on your capacity.

Trusting the Unfolding

Faith in divine timing means trusting that:

- What's for you can't miss you
- The right moment will not pass you by
- The delay may be the miracle in disguise

It's easy to trust when things are going your way.
Harder when you're sitting in uncertainty, watching other people win, wondering if your time will ever come.

But that's when faith becomes real—not just a concept, but a commitment.

A soul whisper that says:

"I trust the unfolding, even when I don't understand it."
"I know the river card will come exactly when it's meant to."
"I'm not behind. I'm being aligned."

The Soul Doesn't Rush

The deepest truth?
Your soul is not in a hurry.

It's not trying to get there faster.
It's trying to get there **truer**.

And divine timing ensures that everything shows up:

- When it's right
- When it's real
- When it's *yours* to receive

So when you've done your part, and nothing's moving—
Don't force it.
Don't chase it.
Don't panic.

Sit in your knowing.
Breathe into your being.
And let the river come to you.

Because sometimes, the greatest act of faith… is not to bet harder, but to wait with peace.

✦ Story Vignette – The River Card – Game Changer or Heartbreaker

Nina had spent years trying to get pregnant. The treatments drained her finances, her energy, and eventually, her marriage. When the divorce was finalized, she gave away the baby clothes she had tucked in the back of her closet and told herself it was time to let go.

Three months later—out of nowhere—she felt off. A random test. A hesitant heartbeat on the monitor. She was pregnant. No doctors, no plans, no explanations.

The river card had turned.

It didn't undo the heartbreak she'd endured, but it reminded her: the game isn't over until it's over. And sometimes, what seems like the end… is just one card away from everything changing.

REFLECTION PROMPT:
The River Card

– Game Changer or Heartbreaker

Have I ever experienced a moment when everything changed in an instant—for better or for worse?

- What did that final "card" reveal about the situation—or about me?
- How do I process outcomes I didn't expect or couldn't control?

The river card doesn't lie—it just reveals.
The power isn't in the outcome... it's in how you choose to respond and rise.

♠ The Table Takeaway

Poker Wisdom

"The river is the moment of truth."
It's the final card. No more betting rounds, no more bluffs, no more chances to improve your hand. Whatever you have now—*that's it.*

The river can be cruel. It can complete your perfect straight... or deliver the one card your opponent needed to crush your dreams.

But that's poker. You play the best you can, and then you let go.

The lesson? **You won't always control the outcome. But you can control how you sit with the result.**

Win or lose, the river teaches acceptance, humility, and grace.

Life Reflection

Life's "river moments" are the ones that close a chapter: the final decision, the diagnosis, the goodbye, the result you can't undo.

It might be a breakthrough—or a heartbreak. A win—or a wake-up call.

This chapter reminds you: You did what you could. The cards fell how they fell. Don't carry blame for things beyond your control.

Sometimes, the real game is learning to hold peace, no matter how the river lands.

Chapter 11: Going All In

Commitment, Soul Purpose, and Big Decisions

There's a defining moment in every game—
The moment when you have to decide:
Do I play it safe?
Or *do I go all in?*

It's not about the hand you're holding anymore.
It's about your **alignment**, your **intuition**, and your **read on the moment**.
It's about trusting yourself enough to risk comfort for something greater.

In life, we face the same pivotal moments—times when we're called to commit more deeply than ever before.
To our path.
To our calling.
To our becoming.

These moments don't come often.
But when they do, they define everything that follows.

Going All In Isn't About Recklessness—it's About Resonance

In poker, going all in is the most vulnerable, high-stakes move.
It means you're no longer hedging.
You're not holding back "just in case."
You're declaring: *"I believe in this. I believe in me."*

And in life, it means the same.

Going all in on your soul path means:

- Choosing your purpose over your fear
- Saying yes to the thing that scares and excites you
- Making decisions based on alignment, not approval
- Putting your whole self on the table—heart, truth, gifts, and voice

You don't go all in *because* it's safe.
You go all in because *you're finally ready.*

Big Decisions: Crossing the Threshold

Some choices are small, daily movements.
But others are thresholds.

Leave the job.
Say yes to the relationship.
Launch the thing.
Move to the city.
Speak the truth.
Walk away from everything that dims you.

These are not just decisions.
They're initiations.

Once you cross the line, you can't go back to who you were.
And you're not supposed to.

Because soul-aligned choices stretch you.
They ask for your full presence.
They burn away everything that was built from fear.

And what's left… is your essence.

Commitment to Soul Purpose

Your soul came here for something specific.
Not just to survive.
Not just to follow the script.
But to embody a *frequency*, to deliver a *message*, to live a *truth*.

You may not know every step.
You may not have every answer.
But deep down, you already feel the *direction.*

And commitment doesn't mean perfection.
It means showing up anyway.
Again and again.
Especially when you're scared.
Especially when it would be easier to fold.

When you go all in on your purpose, the universe starts meeting you there.
Opportunities align.
People appear.
Synchronicities increase.
And your life begins to reflect your truth.

Going all in isn't about the outcome—it's about the alignment.
It's not about being fearless—it's about being faithful.
It's not about having the perfect hand—it's about trusting yourself enough to play it with your whole heart.

Moments When You Risk Everything— and Grow

There comes a moment in every soul-led life when the stakes rise.
You're standing at the edge of what's familiar, what's safe, what's known…
And your spirit whispers:

"It's time."

You may feel unprepared.
The timing may feel off.
The outcome may be unclear.
But everything in your being is calling you forward—
Not to play it safe, but to *risk it all… and rise.*

These are the sacred moments when you go all in.
Not with certainty—
But with conviction.

Growth Comes After the Leap

When you risk everything—your comfort, your certainty, your reputation, your patterns—
you step into a space where growth is *guaranteed*, even if success isn't.

Because risking everything doesn't mean you lose it.
It means you're willing to let go of the version of you that was never fully alive.

Growth doesn't happen in theory.
It happens in:

- The phone call you were terrified to make
- The truth you finally said out loud
- The healing session you decided to lead, not just study
- The move, the investment, the YES that changed everything

You can prepare forever.
But you grow the moment you stop rehearsing and start *living* it.

Fear Is the Gatekeeper to Expansion

In poker, going all in puts your chips—and your ego—on the line.
In life, going all in puts your *identity* on the line.

It forces you to meet fear eye-to-eye and say:

"Even if I lose everything I thought I needed... I'll find a version of myself I've never met before."

And that version?
Is *closer to your truth* than anything you've ever known.

Because on the other side of fear is always freedom.
Not the freedom of having it all figured out—
But the freedom of no longer playing small.

You May Not Win Immediately—But You Will Emerge Transformed

Sometimes, going all in doesn't bring instant results.
You may still face rejection, delays, confusion, or setbacks.

But here's the secret:

You grow in the act of leaping.
In the courage it takes to let go.
In the faith it takes to move with no guarantee.

Every time you risk everything for your soul's truth, you build a
deeper trust within.
And that trust becomes the foundation of your next becoming.

You grow the moment you stop playing to protect your past
and start playing to honor your future.

So when the moment comes…
When life places that sacred invitation in front of you…
Don't just sit there second-guessing.

Take a deep breath.
Feel the fear.
And go all in.

✦ Story Vignette – Going All In

Marcos had a stable job in finance, a sleek condo, and a perfectly curated life. But every night, he sketched tattoos in his notebook, dreaming of opening a studio that fused art with healing—ink with intention.

He told no one at first. Not even his partner. *Who gives up six figures for... tattoos?*

Then came the moment. He had saved enough. Found a studio space. A friend offered to invest. The only thing left... was the leap.

Quitting was terrifying. Opening day felt like freefall. But when his first client cried in the chair—healing through the design they'd co-created—Marcos knew:
He hadn't gambled.
He had *trusted*.

Going all in wasn't reckless.
It was sacred.

REFLECTION PROMPT:
Going All In

What area of my life is calling me to commit more fully—with my whole heart?

- Am I holding back out of fear, uncertainty, or past disappointment?
- What would it look like to trust my soul's purpose enough to go all in?

Going all in isn't reckless—it's reverent.
It's a sacred yes to the life that's waiting on the other side of hesitation.

♠ The Table Takeaway

Poker Wisdom

"When you go all in, there's no turning back."
It's the boldest move in poker. You push all your chips into the pot, betting everything on one hand. It's not about luck alone—it's about conviction, timing, and reading the table.

Sometimes it's a power play. Sometimes it's a desperate act. Either way, it's a declaration: *"This is it. I'm committed."*

The lesson? **Going all in isn't about recklessness—it's about *clarity.***
You've sized up the risk. You've chosen your moment. Now you're standing behind it.

You can't win big if you never push in your stack.

Life Reflection

In life, "all in" moments define us—those times you risk your comfort, your reputation, or your heart because *something bigger* is calling.

Starting a business. Leaving a toxic relationship. Saying yes to your purpose.

It's terrifying. It's exhilarating. And it changes everything.

This chapter invites you to ask:
Where are you holding back out of fear?
And what might happen if you finally pushed all your chips into you?

Part IV:
Luck, Losses & Lessons

Suit: Diamonds
Symbolism: Value, purpose, wealth (inner and outer), and clarity.

Chapter 12: Beginner's Luck and Divine Grace

Times When Things Work Out for No Logical Reason

There are moments in life that simply defy explanation.

You walk into a room for the first time… and meet the exact person you needed.
You take a leap with no experience… and land in the perfect place.
You say yes to something your mind can't justify… and doors fly open.
You show up unprepared… and still win the hand.

These moments are not strategy.
They're not hustle.
They're not logic.

They are grace.
Or what the world likes to call: *beginner's luck.*

What Is Beginner's Luck, Really?

In poker, beginner's luck is when a new player—unskilled, inexperienced, unaware of the risks—walks in and wins big.
They play boldly because they don't know the odds.
They trust their gut because they haven't been trained to overthink.
They move with freedom because they don't yet carry the weight of fear.

And the same thing happens in life.

Sometimes, things work out beautifully not because you had it all figured out…
But because you were still open.
Still innocent enough to believe.
Still connected to possibility instead of pressure.

Beginner's luck is not random.
It's a brief window where your energy is so *clear*—so unguarded, so unburdened—that the universe can move through you without resistance.

Grace Doesn't Follow Logic—It Follows Alignment

There will be times when everything you've learned says *no*, but your intuition says *yes.*
And when you follow that yes, doors open that logic would've never unlocked.

That's grace.

When you:

- Arrive late and still get the seat
- Forget the script and deliver something more real
- Miss the opportunity… only to discover the *right one* was waiting

Grace has its own rhythm.
It shows up for the ones willing to move from soul, not ego.
It favors the open-hearted, the faithful, the bold.

And sometimes, the miracle isn't that it worked—
It's that you were *willing to try at all.*

You Don't Have to Earn Everything

This is where divine grace departs from the rules of the game.

You don't always have to earn your blessings through sweat
and suffering.
You don't always have to "deserve" the win.
Sometimes, Spirit just decides:

"Here. You're ready. Even if you don't think you are."

That's when the healing lands.
That's when the opportunity finds you.
That's when you realize… you are being loved beyond logic.

Beginner's luck isn't just a fluke.
It's a glimpse of what life feels like when you stop gripping and
start flowing.
When you stop proving… and start receiving.

Universal Support, Angels, and Intuition

If you've ever felt something helping you when no one was physically there—
If you've ever walked into a moment that felt orchestrated from above—
If you've ever received a message, a knowing, a whisper, a sign that stopped you in your tracks—

Then you've experienced unseen support.

Call it angels.
Call it Spirit.
Call it the universe, the Divine, the higher self.
The name doesn't matter as much as the *presence.*

Because when life aligns in ways you couldn't have planned—
When answers show up before the question is even fully formed—
That's more than luck.
That's guidance.

You Are Never Truly Playing Alone

In poker, the game appears to be you versus them.
A table full of opponents.
Everyone for themselves.

But in life, you are never just one soul alone in the game.
You are surrounded—supported by energies, beings, and guidance that want your highest good.

The thing is, they don't override your will.
They wait for your openness.

They speak in symbols, feelings, nudges—so gentle you could miss them if you're distracted by doubt.

They come through your **intuition**—
That inner signal that whispers, *"Yes, this way."*
The gut feeling that says, *"No, not here."*

And the more you listen…
The louder that guidance becomes.

Angels Speak in Energy, Not Just Words

Whether or not you "see" angels, you've likely felt them:

- That wave of peace that fills the room in a time of chaos
- That spark of courage in your chest when you needed to act
- That warmth in your body during meditation or prayer
- The song, number, feather, phrase, or dream that came at *just* the right time

This is how Spirit speaks—
Soft, but precise.
Invisible, but unmistakable.

You don't have to understand how it works.
You just have to **open to it.**

Your Intuition Is the Bridge to the Unseen

The deeper you trust your intuition, the more you begin to notice the presence of support all around you.
You stop doubting every decision.
You stop needing signs to be thunderclaps.
You begin to live from an inner compass instead of outer noise.

You realize:

- *"I'm not crazy—I'm connected."*
- *"I'm not alone—I'm guided."*
- *"I don't need to control everything—because I'm supported in ways I can't always see."*

This is the real grace.
Not just things working out—but the quiet knowing that
you're never navigating this life without help.

Divine grace walks with you.
Angels play at your table.
And your intuition is the language they use to lead you home.

✦ Story Vignette – Beginner's Luck and Divine Grace

Layla had never hiked a day in her life. She was just tagging along with friends who promised "an easy walk." Halfway up the trail, a wrong turn led her to a clearing she hadn't meant to find. The sun broke through the trees. A hawk soared above her. And in that moment—no sound, no goal, no pressure—she felt something crack open inside.

She sat on a rock and wept without knowing why. It wasn't sadness. It was release. And knowing.

Three months later, she quit her job, enrolled in an herbal medicine course, and started guiding women's healing circles in the forest.

It wasn't logic. It was grace.
And it all started with a trail she wasn't supposed to take.

REFLECTION PROMPT:
Beginner's Luck and Divine Grace

When was a time something worked out for me in a way I couldn't have planned or predicted?

- How did that moment make me feel—grateful, humbled, supported?
- What if grace is always available, not just when I feel "ready" or "worthy"?

Some blessings defy logic.
They remind us we're never playing this game alone.

♠ The Table Takeaway

Poker Wisdom

"Sometimes the new player catches the river and wins the whole pot."
Beginner's luck isn't just folklore—it's real. New players often defy logic, make bold plays, and walk away with wins that seasoned pros never saw coming.

It can be frustrating. But it's also humbling. Because poker, like life, isn't always about mastery. Sometimes it's about openness. Fresh eyes. Unburdened energy.

The seasoned player may have skill—but the beginner has nothing to prove and nothing to lose. And that freedom? It opens unexpected doors.

The lesson?
Stay open to the miraculous. Grace shows up when—and where—you least expect it.

Life Reflection

Have you ever had something work out that you couldn't explain?
A job landed. A connection formed. A dream realized. And you weren't "qualified."

That's grace. That's Spirit showing off.

This chapter reminds you that logic isn't the only force at play. Faith, flow, and alignment are powerful allies.

Your breakthrough might not come from grinding.
It might come from trusting the hand you didn't even know how to play.

Chapter 13: Tilt — When Emotions Run the Show

Emotional Regulation, Shadow Work, and Reactivity

In poker, there's a term called *tilt*.

It happens when a player loses emotional control—after a bad beat, a frustrating hand, or a long streak of losses.
Their frustration builds. Their ego flares.
They start making poor decisions, not because they lack skill…
But because they've stopped playing with clarity—and started reacting from emotion.

In life, we experience *tilt* too.

We lash out in an argument.
We spiral after a disappointment.
We ghost someone we love.
We overreact, shut down, explode, retreat, or overcompensate…

Not because we're bad people—
But because we're emotionally dysregulated.
And our inner wounds—the ones we thought we buried—are now running the game.

Emotions Are Not the Enemy

Emotions are sacred.
They're messengers.
They tell you what you value, what's unhealed, what's been ignored.

But emotions are *not* meant to drive the car.
They're meant to ride in the passenger seat—seen, heard, acknowledged... but not steering.

Emotional regulation is the ability to:

- Pause before reacting
- Breathe when you want to scream
- Name what you feel without becoming what you feel
- Stay rooted in truth, even when emotion rises like a storm

It's not about suppressing how you feel.
It's about staying conscious enough to choose your response instead of acting from your wound.

Shadow Work: Facing the Parts You've Rejected

Tilt isn't just about surface-level stress.
It's what happens when our shadow takes the wheel.

The shadow is the part of you that holds:

- Old pain you never processed
- Childhood beliefs you never questioned
- Rage, shame, jealousy, grief—unacknowledged and unintegrated

When triggered, these shadows flood the system.
And suddenly you're not responding as your present self.
You're reacting as the *unhealed version* of you—the one who
was abandoned, betrayed, unheard, or unloved.

Shadow work is the process of turning toward those parts
instead of exiling them.
It's looking at your emotional triggers and asking:

"Where is this coming from?"
"What part of me is crying out?"
"What does this feeling need in order to heal?"

You don't heal your shadow by pretending it's not there.
You heal it by bringing it into the light—with compassion.

The Game Doesn't End Because You Tilt—But You Must Recenter

In poker, a player on tilt rarely wins.
But that doesn't mean they're out forever.

With self-awareness, they can pause.
Breathe.
Regroup.
Reconnect with the flow of the game.

In life, the same applies.

Your spiritual work isn't about *never* tilting.
It's about recognizing it faster, staying curious instead of self-
punishing, and returning to presence.

Your power doesn't come from being perfectly composed.
It comes from being willing to look at your emotional landscape
honestly—and lovingly.

Your emotions are sacred, but they are not your identity. Your shadow holds wisdom, but it does not hold the steering wheel.

And your healing happens not when you feel nothing—
But when you feel fully… and still choose with clarity.

Healing from Loss, Frustration, and Burnout

There's a particular kind of *tilt* that doesn't come from one single moment—

It comes from **accumulation.**

Loss upon loss.
Frustration on top of frustration.
Trying, giving, showing up—again and again—only to feel like it's never enough.
And somewhere along the way, you don't just feel tired…

You feel *disconnected from yourself.*

That's not just emotional fatigue.
That's **burnout**—body, mind, and soul.

Loss: The Silent Grief That Lingers

Loss doesn't always announce itself dramatically.
Sometimes it arrives quietly:

- The dream you let go of
- The version of yourself you outgrew
- The friend who drifted
- The job that cost you your joy
- The "almost" that never became

Loss isn't just about death—it's about **what didn't last.**
And when we don't grieve it properly, it builds beneath the surface.

Suddenly, one small thing—one disappointment, one rejection—breaks the dam.
And we tilt.

But the healing begins when you finally *allow yourself to feel the loss fully.*
To name it.
To cry over it.
To bless it for what it gave you—and release it for what it couldn't.

Loss processed with love becomes wisdom.
Loss suppressed becomes rage, numbness, or shutdown.

Frustration: When the Path Feels Blocked

You've done the work.
You've said the affirmations.
You've followed your guidance.

But nothing is changing.
Or worse, it seems like everyone else is winning while you're stuck in limbo.

Frustration is valid.
But if left unspoken, it festers into resentment—toward life, others, or yourself.

Healing frustration begins with *acknowledging it without shame.*

You can say:

- "I'm angry this hasn't shifted yet."
- "I'm tired of waiting."

- "I feel let down by life right now."

Let that truth breathe.

And then remember:
Frustration is not a stop sign.
It's a signal to pause, realign, and possibly reroute.

Sometimes what you're reaching for *isn't blocked*—it's just asking you to meet it from a deeper version of yourself.

Burnout: When the Spirit Is Starved

Burnout is not just tiredness.
It's what happens when you've been in constant output—emotionally, mentally, spiritually—without enough nourishment.

You've been strong for too long.
Holding space. Keeping the peace. Carrying the weight.

And now your soul is whispering:

"I can't keep running on empty."

Healing from burnout doesn't come from a vacation or a nap—though those help.
It comes from restoring your relationship with yourself.

Ask:

- Where have I abandoned myself in the name of performance or productivity?
- What am I craving that I've been too busy to receive?

- What part of me is trying to be everything for everyone—and at what cost?

The antidote to burnout is reconnection.
To your body.
To your boundaries.
To your joy.
To your *why*.

Your Healing Is Sacred—and Deserves Time

You can't rush your way out of tilt.
You can't bypass your emotions to "get back in the game."

True healing requires slowness.
Presence.
And gentleness with the parts of you that have tried so hard to hold it all together.

You don't need to be fixed.
You need to be *felt*.
Witnessed. Supported. Loved.

And the moment you begin to meet yourself with compassion instead of criticism—
That's when the healing begins.

You will rise again—
Not because you pushed through…
But because you paused long enough to return to yourself.

✦ Story Vignette – Tilt – When Emotions Run the Show

Jared prided himself on being level-headed. Calm under pressure. The guy everyone trusted to keep it together.

Until the day his business deal crumbled.

He'd sunk everything into it—time, money, reputation. When the email came in that it had fallen through, something in him snapped. He shouted at the barista. Slammed his laptop shut so hard it cracked. Drove three hours without knowing where he was going.

He was in *tilt*—the poker term for when emotion hijacks logic, and every move becomes reaction, not intention.

It took a full breakdown—and a quiet talk with his sister—for him to admit it: he'd been avoiding grief, not just disappointment.

Losing the deal didn't break him.
Ignoring his emotions nearly did.

REFLECTION PROMPT:
Tilt—When Emotions Run the Show

What situations or people tend to throw me off balance
emotionally?

- What deeper wound or belief might those reactions be
  pointing to?
- How can I respond with awareness, rather than react out
  of old pain?

Your emotions aren't the enemy—they're messengers.
Learning to listen without being ruled by them is a mark of true
mastery.

♠ The Table Takeaway

Poker Wisdom

"Play the player, not the hand—but don't let emotions play you."
Every poker player knows the danger of going on tilt. One bad beat, one careless call, and suddenly your emotions hijack your strategy. You chase losses, make rash moves, and burn through your stack—not because of the cards, but because of the chaos in your head.

Tilt turns skill into sabotage.

The pros? They know how to breathe. To reset. To walk away before the next hand costs more than just chips.

The lesson?
Emotional regulation is as essential as knowing the odds.
Stay cool. Or you'll pay for the heat.

Life Reflection

Life will provoke you. People will push buttons you didn't know you had. Circumstances will shake your center.

What you do next? That's everything.

This chapter is your reminder:
Pause before you react.
Learn your emotional triggers.
Protect your peace like it's your last chip.

When emotions run the show, wisdom walks out the door.
But when you master your inner game, no external chaos can break your stride.

Chapter 14: Reading the Signs

How Spirit Shows Up: Signs, Symbols, and Numbers

Sometimes the next move isn't written in the cards—
It's whispered through signs.

You're asking for guidance.
Praying for clarity.
Trying to decide whether to fold, go all in, or simply hold your place at the table…

And then, just as doubt creeps in, something appears:

- A feather on your path
- Repeating numbers like 11:11 or 222
- A stranger's words that echo what you've been thinking
- A song, a dream, or a line in a book that speaks *directly to your soul*

This is how Spirit speaks.
Not always loudly.
Not always obviously.
But *always intentionally.*

Signs Are Love Notes from the Unseen

Spirit doesn't force its way into your life.
It invites you into conversation.
And signs are the sacred language of that conversation.

They arrive in moments of synchronicity, subtle knowing, and perfect timing—not to control you, but to remind you that you are *not walking this path alone.*

You are supported.
You are seen.
You are being guided.

Even when you can't see the full hand—Spirit is already five steps ahead, nudging you with grace.

Symbols That Speak to the Soul

Symbols carry frequency.
They bypass the logical mind and land straight in the heart.

A butterfly might show up just when you're contemplating transformation.
A hawk when you're being asked to see from a higher perspective.
A rose when you're healing through love or grief.
A snake when you're shedding the old version of you.

Spirit often uses personal symbolism—images and messages that *you* will recognize, even if no one else does.

Pay attention to:

- Animal messengers
- Elemental energies (wind, fire, rain)
- Colors or objects that repeat

- Dreams that stay with you
- Gut feelings that say, *"This means something."*

Your soul speaks in symbols.
And Spirit responds in kind.

Numbers as Divine Codes

Numbers are among the most common spiritual signs—and they come with frequency and meaning:

- 111 – New beginnings, alignment with purpose
- 222 – Balance, faith, trust in the process
- 333 – Support from Spirit, especially from ascended guides
- 444 – Protection, grounding, angelic presence
- 555 – Change is here; embrace the shift
- 777 – Spiritual awakening, divine insight
- 888 – Abundance and karmic balance
- 999 – Completion, cycles closing, making space for the new

When you keep seeing the same numbers over and over, it's not coincidence.
It's communication.
It's Spirit letting you know: *"Yes, you're on the right track. Keep going."*

How to Receive More Signs

You don't have to chase signs.
You simply have to be *open to receiving them.*

Try this:

- Begin your day by asking: *"Spirit, please show me a clear sign today."*
- Don't overanalyze. Stay open. Stay present.
- Notice what shows up in your environment, emotions, conversations, or dreams.
- Ask, *"What is this showing me about where I'm being guided?"*

You'll start to notice more—because Spirit has always been speaking.

You're just now learning how to listen.

Signs are not magic tricks.
They are invitations to trust.
They are Spirit's way of reminding you:
You are never playing this hand alone.

Spiritual Awareness as a Skill Set

Spiritual awareness isn't just a gift—
It's a skill.
One that you can nurture, refine, and deepen over time.

Just like a seasoned poker player learns to read the room,
observe patterns, and trust their instincts...
A spiritually aware person learns to read the *energy* behind the experience.
To sense the lesson beneath the chaos.
To hear the whisper beneath the noise.

This doesn't happen all at once.
It grows through devotion, attention, and practice.

Awareness Begins with Presence

You can't read the signs if you're moving too fast.
You can't feel guidance if you're numb from distraction.
You can't hear Spirit if your mind is louder than your soul.

That's why spiritual awareness begins with one thing:
presence.

It's the ability to slow down, become still, and ask:

- *What's actually happening here?*
- *Is this mine, or am I absorbing someone else's energy?*
- *What is life trying to show me in this moment?*

Awareness isn't just about mystical visions.
It's about subtle attunement.
A growing sensitivity to energy, emotion, and truth.

Skill Comes Through Practice

You build spiritual awareness the same way you build any muscle:

- By showing up daily.
- By paying attention to the unseen.
- By journaling your dreams, synchronicities, and intuitive hits.
- By meditating, grounding, and asking clear questions.
- By *trusting yourself more each time you're right—and learning when you're not.*

You don't need to "be psychic" to be aware.
You just need to stay curious and committed.

Over time, what once felt invisible becomes obvious.
You begin to *feel* when energy shifts.
You sense who to trust.
You know when to move—and when to wait.
You start playing the game of life not just with logic, but with inner knowing.

Spiritual Awareness Protects and Empowers You

The more aware you are:

- The less reactive you become
- The fewer mistakes you make based on fear
- The more peace you carry—even in uncertainty
- The stronger your boundaries, your decisions, your alignment

You stop needing signs to be loud.
You start hearing them in silence.

And that… is where your true power lives.

Spiritual awareness is not just knowing that you are guided—
It's walking through the world as if that's true.
It's choosing to live not by default, but by divine design.

"The only way to discover the limits of the possible is to go beyond them into the impossible."
— Arthur C. Clarke

✦ Story Vignette – Reading the Signs

Every morning, Ana pulled the same tarot card: *The Tower*. Sudden change. Upheaval. She brushed it off—just a fluke. But then her dreams turned stormy. Lights flickered in her apartment. And that gut feeling she kept pushing down? It grew louder.

At work, she'd been ignoring the burnout. The subtle disrespect. The knowing that she was meant for something else.

Then, one rainy afternoon, her manager "accidentally" copied her on an email. They were planning to replace her.

Ana didn't rage. She didn't beg.
She'd already seen the signs.

The next morning, she woke up, made coffee, and started designing her own intuitive coaching business.

When you read the signs early,
you don't need the Universe to scream.

REFLECTION PROMPT:
Reading the Signs

What signs, numbers, symbols, or synchronicities have I noticed lately?

- How did they make me feel—and what might they be trying to tell me?
- Am I open to receiving subtle guidance, even if it doesn't come the way I expect?

The Universe is always speaking.
The question is: are you quiet enough to hear... and brave enough to follow?

♠ The Table Takeaway

Poker Wisdom

"A tell doesn't lie—even when the player does."
In poker, not all truths are spoken. A twitch of the lip, a tapping finger, a sudden stillness—these are tells. Subtle clues that reveal more than the cards ever will. Great players don't just play the hand—they read the room.

It's not about psychic power.
It's about presence. Observation. Intuition honed into skill.

The best reads come from silence and attention—not force.
You learn to listen with your eyes.

The lesson?
Signals are always there.
You just have to know what to look for—and when to trust what you see.

Life Reflection

Life sends signals too:
A strange dream.
An unease around someone new.
A coincidence that's just a little *too* perfect.

Call them signs, synchronicities, or soul whispers.
When you start paying attention, you'll notice: life *wants* to be read.

This chapter reminds you to stay alert—not paranoid, but perceptive.
Your intuition is your tell detector.
Use it wisely. Trust it fully.

Chapter 15: House Rules & Universal Law

Karma, Spiritual Law, and Cause and Effect

Every poker game has its house rules.
They might vary from place to place, but they define what's allowed, what's fair, and what will get you removed from the table.
Whether you understand the rules or not—they still apply.
And if you ignore them, you'll eventually pay the price.

Life operates under spiritual laws in much the same way.

These aren't human-made systems.
They aren't rules built to control you.
They are *cosmic principles*—neutral, exact, and deeply fair.

You can't cheat them. But when you align with them, life flows in harmony. When you violate them—knowingly or not—life becomes friction, confusion, and delay.

And the most well-known of these laws is karma.

What Karma Is (and Isn't)

Karma is not punishment.
It's not some spiritual scoreboard where good people win and bad people lose.
Karma is a law of cause and effect—pure and impersonal.

What you put out returns.
What you choose ripples.
Your energy, your words, your actions—they all plant seeds.
And eventually, you harvest the fruit of those seeds.

If you plant love, generosity, and truth—you receive more of the same.
If you plant fear, manipulation, or avoidance—those too will return, in ways that ask for healing or clarity.

Karma is not *retribution.*
It's *correction*—a universal balancing system that ensures what's out of alignment will eventually be brought back to truth.

Spiritual Laws Are Always in Play

Whether you believe in them or not, spiritual laws operate 24/7.

Some of the most essential include:

- The Law of Vibration: Everything is energy. What you are energetically aligned with is what you attract.
- The Law of Resonance: Like attracts like. Your internal frequency mirrors your external reality.

- **The Law of Reciprocity:** What you give returns—not always from the same source, but always in the right form.
- **The Law of Free Will:** You are not controlled by fate—you are given choice, again and again.
- **The Law of Growth:** What isn't healed will be repeated until it's understood and integrated.
- **The Law of Detachment:** When you let go of clinging, flow is restored. Control blocks miracles.

When you play by these laws, you don't just "win" the game of life—you start co-creating it in harmony with divine intelligence.

Your Life Is Not Random—It's a Mirror

If something keeps showing up in your life—
The same kind of person, pattern, pain, or struggle—
It's not bad luck.
It's karmic momentum.

The good news?
You're not a victim of karma.

You're an editor of it—moment by moment, through your awareness, your choices, and your energy.

You can shift the game any time you choose:

- By choosing forgiveness over resentment
- By acting in integrity instead of fear
- By slowing down and reflecting instead of reacting
- By seeing the lesson instead of only the loss

Playing in Alignment with Spiritual Law

When you play poker and understand the house rules, you're empowered to make better choices.
You know what's fair, what's not, and how to stay in the flow of the game.

The same goes for life.

When you align with spiritual law:

- You feel less confusion and more clarity
- You stop forcing and start flowing
- You trust the process instead of trying to control the outcome
- You begin to experience synchronicity, grace, and peace—even during challenge

This is when the "game" becomes sacred.
Not about winning or losing…
But about becoming more conscious, more heart-led, more soul-aligned with every move you make.

Karma isn't keeping score.
It's keeping you on course.
And when you understand the laws behind the game…
You stop fearing the consequences—
And start co-creating your destiny.

You Can't Cheat Life—But You Can Align With It

Some people treat life like a hustle.
They try to skip steps, manipulate outcomes, or copy someone else's path to success.
And for a while, it might even look like it's working.

But just like in poker, short-term wins don't last when they come from misalignment.

Eventually, the house catches up.
Not out of punishment—
But out of principle.

Because life isn't something you can cheat.
It's something you're meant to *honor*.

You're here to play in alignment with your soul's truth.
Not with fear.
Not with ego.
Not with projection or performance.

But with clarity.
With love.
With trust in the deeper rhythm guiding it all.

When you play in alignment:

- You trust the timing instead of forcing it
- You release attachment and open to flow
- You choose actions that match your integrity—even when no one is watching
- You stop chasing wins and start living from wholeness

You can't fake your energy.
And you can't bypass your soul.

But you *can* align.
You *can* return to your truth.
You *can* surrender the hustle and embrace the harmony.

And when you do, life becomes something more than just a game.

It becomes a sacred exchange—
Where what you give is returned,
Where what you believe is reflected,
And where what you align with becomes your reality.

No, you can't cheat life.
But you can listen to it.
Align with it.
And play it in a way that makes your soul proud.

✦ Story Vignette – House Rules & Universal Law

Tariq worked in corporate law, where winning meant everything—and loopholes were the game. He got clients off the hook with finesse. Reputation: pristine. Bank account: overflowing.

But inside, something gnawed at him. One case in particular: he'd defended a company that buried evidence of environmental damage. He did his job. Played by the rules. And won.

Six months later, his teenage daughter came home from a protest—tears in her eyes—holding a photo of a polluted river. "How could anyone *do* this?" she asked.

He couldn't answer. Not honestly.

That night, he stayed up reading about karma, truth, and integrity—not by man's measure, but the soul's.

The next day, he quit. Not because he lost.
But because he finally understood:
The House has rules.
But the Universe has laws.

REFLECTION PROMPT:
House Rules & Universal Law

Where in my life am I being invited to align more deeply with my truth and values?

- Are there areas where I've been bending the rules—internally or externally—to "win"?
- What would it look like to live in harmony with spiritual law, rather than trying to work around it?

You don't have to cheat the game when you're aligned with the highest version of yourself.
Karma isn't punishment—it's the pattern. And you have the power to choose a new one.

♠ The Table Takeaway

Poker Wisdom

"You can't argue with the house rules."
Every poker room has its own rules—posted or unspoken. You might not agree with them. You might wish they were different. But if you want to stay in the game, you play by them—or you leave the table.

Smart players don't waste energy resisting the structure.
They *learn* the rules.
They *adapt* their strategy.
They *respect* the game.

The difference between amateurs and pros?
Pros know when a rule is rigid—and when it's just a norm they can work around.

The lesson?
Master the system, and you gain power.
Resist it blindly, and you just bleed chips.

Life Reflection

Life also has rules: not just human-made laws, **but spiritual laws**—like karma, cause and effect, energy exchange, divine timing.
You can't cheat these. You can work with them.

When you understand the universal laws, life flows more smoothly.
You realize that alignment is more effective than force.

CHAPTER 16: One More Hand

When You Stay Too Long at the Table

Every poker player knows the feeling.

You're ahead. Stacked. Riding a hot streak. You told yourself you'd walk away once you doubled up—but here you are, still sitting, still playing.

Just one more hand.

And then another.

And then… you misread a bluff. Tilted a little. Overplayed a marginal hand.

Before you know it, half your stack is gone. Then all of it.

It's not bad luck. It's bad timing—and attachment.

The Truth About Leaving While Ahead

Walking away when you're up is one of the hardest disciplines in poker. Not because it's technically difficult, but because it challenges ego, greed, and the human tendency to chase more.

- What if the next hand is even better?
- What if I'm just getting started?
- What if I leave and regret it?

But the pros know: **timing is everything**.

When you don't honor the natural ebb and flow of the game, you start playing against the rhythm instead of with it. You stop making clear, sharp decisions—and start playing from grasping and fear.

The lesson?

Every hot streak has an expiration. And wisdom lies in knowing when your moment has passed—and being brave enough to let it go.

Life Has Its Own Exit Points

This isn't just about poker.

It's about life.

It's the job you've outgrown but are afraid to leave.

The relationship that once fit but now feels hollow.

The success that came, but now feels like a gilded cage.

Like poker, life gives us "exit points"—moments when the energy shifts and we're called to move on. And just like at the table, we often ignore them.

Because we're afraid.

Afraid of losing what we've gained.

Afraid of change.

Afraid that the next table won't be as good as this one.

But when we stay too long at a table where our energy no longer belongs, we don't just stall. We decline.

Burnout. Resentment. Repeating lessons. Losing clarity.

The win starts to feel like a weight.

The Spiritual Law of Detachment

Spiritually speaking, this is where the Law of Detachment comes into play.

This law teaches us:

- You don't cling to the outcome.
- You let go of what's complete.
- You trust the next hand—before you've seen the cards.

Detachment doesn't mean apathy. It means faith.

It means recognizing when you've harvested the fruit of a season—and having the courage to plant a new one.

It means honoring your wins without overplaying them into losses.

It means listening to your soul, not your fear of scarcity.

Because when you walk away aligned—with timing, clarity, and trust—you make room for what's next.

And life always deals again.

What's at Stake When You Stay Too Long

When you ignore the signs to leave, you end up playing defense.

You start making poor decisions out of habit or pride.

You defend your seat instead of following your path.

You forget that life is always moving—and you're meant to move with it.

But when you listen—when you recognize the "one more hand" moment and bow out with grace—you preserve not just your resources...

You preserve your soul alignment.

Honor the Chapter That's Closing

Every win has its closing bell. Every season has its final hand.

The question is: will you hear it?

And will you have the discipline—and the trust—to leave when it's time?

Because the universe rewards those who honor flow.

When you walk away aligned, the next table is always waiting.

One with fresh cards.

New lessons. And perhaps—your greatest win yet.

✦ Story Vignette – One More Hand

Darren had doubled his chips in under an hour.

He was in flow—reading the table, playing smart, calling bluffs like a psychic. The other players were rattled. Even the dealer smirked as Darren raked in pot after pot. He texted his brother: *"I'm on fire. Feels like the universe is dealing me aces."*

But then came the voice—the one every gambler hears at least once.

"Just one more hand…"

He played it. And another. Then the tides shifted.

A slow bleed. One beat. Then a bluff gone wrong. He didn't see it coming until he was pot-committed and trapped. Half his stack vanished. Pride flared. He stayed. Tried to win it back. But the table had changed, and he hadn't.

By midnight, he walked out with empty pockets—and a heavy lesson.

REFLECTION PROMPT:
One More Hand

Where in your life are you lingering too long at the table?

Is it a job, relationship, habit, or identity that once served you—but now drains you?

What are you afraid you'll lose if you walk away… and what might you gain?

If you trusted that the next hand life deals could be even better—would you finally fold this one?

♠ The Table Takeaway

Poker Wisdom

"The longer you stay at a hot table, the colder your odds become."
Success feels invincible—until it isn't. At the table, winning can breed overconfidence. You forget the odds. You ignore the shifting rhythm. The very hand you celebrated becomes your downfall.

Pros know when to quit *while ahead*. It takes discipline, not bravado. You win. You cash out. You honor the flow.

Sometimes the best move is walking away—not because you're losing, but because you're *no longer aligned* with the table's energy.

Life Reflection

There are seasons where everything clicks: love flows, business thrives, healing accelerates. But ego whispers, *"Keep going. Don't leave. You've finally got it."*

That's when spiritual maturity says: *Pause. Evaluate. Walk away* on purpose.

Success isn't meant to be hoarded—it's meant to be honored. Just because you can keep going doesn't mean you should. Know when the season has served you.

The next hand—your *next chapter*—might be even better.

Conclusion: Life's a Game—But You're More Than a Player

Final Message of Empowerment and Purpose

You've played the hands.
You've faced the turns.
You've felt the sting of loss and the rush of intuition.
You've stayed in the game even when it felt unfair, uncertain, or impossible.

And now, here you are—wiser. Clearer. Rooted in something deeper than strategy or luck.

Because this book was never really about poker.
It was about *you*.
And the way you choose to show up in the unfolding game of life.

You're not just reacting to what life deals you.
You are co-creating with every move you make.
With every boundary you hold.
With every dream you follow.

With every moment you choose presence over panic, alignment over fear.

That is your power.

Not to control the outcome—
But to **show up as your highest self** no matter the hand.

You may not get to shuffle the deck.
But you *do* get to:

- Trust your intuition
- Set your own pace
- Say yes when it's time to go all in
- Say no when something doesn't feel right
- Walk away with grace
- Stay with love
- Fold the old story
- And rise into your becoming

This isn't about winning or losing.
This is about **awakening.**

To your soul. To your gifts. To your truth.
To your divine role in the great unfolding.

So take everything you've learned—every insight, every reminder, every tool—and carry it with you like your lucky charm.

Not because you need luck—
But because you now walk with **clarity.** With **faith.** With **purpose.** You don't just play the game anymore.

You know who you are at the table.
And that... changes everything.

You're Not Just Playing the Game—
You're Co-Creating It

Every choice you make sends a ripple through the unseen.
Every intention you hold plants a seed in the field of possibility.
Every time you pause, realign, and choose love over fear—you
rewrite the rules of your own destiny.

You were never here just to survive the game.
You came to **transform it.**
To infuse the ordinary with sacredness.
To take your seat at the table as a soul who knows her worth,
trusts her intuition, and plays with purpose.

You are not a passive player.
You are a co-creator with Spirit.

So play boldly.
Live fully.
And never forget: the real win was never in the cards...

It's in the way you played the game—with soul, with courage,
and with unshakable faith in who you are becoming.

✦ Story Vignette – Life's a Game—But You're More Than a Player

Maya sat at a friend's poker night, more for the wine than the game. She'd always said she didn't "get" poker. Too many rules. Too much bluffing.

But as the cards were dealt, she noticed something. How each player held themselves. Who played safe. Who took wild risks. Who folded too soon. Who always thought the next hand would fix everything.

It hit her: this wasn't about cards. It never had been.

It was about mindset. Energy. Intuition. Timing.
It was about how people showed up—at the table, in life.

She looked down at her hand. Not great. Not terrible. But hers to play.

And suddenly, she realized:
She wasn't just here to react to life.
She was here to *co-create* it.

REFLECTION PROMPT:
Life's a Game

—But You're More Than a Player

What am I now ready to own, release, or embody—knowing that I'm not just playing the game, I'm co-creating it?

- How has my understanding of life, choice, and intuition shifted through these chapters?
- What soul-aligned action can I take today that reflects who I'm becoming?

This is more than reflection—it's initiation.
You've seen behind the cards. Now it's time to play from your truth.

♠ The Table Takeaway

Poker Wisdom

"In the end, it's not just about playing your cards—it's about playing *yourself*."
The best poker players don't just read the odds. They read the table. They know when to fold, when to call, when to bluff— and when to go all in.

But here's the deeper truth:
They're not just playing cards.
They're mastering patience, discipline, timing, intuition, emotional control, and risk.
They're sharpening life skills through a deck of 52.

The real game? It's not poker.
It's who you become while playing it.

Life Reflection

Life deals the cards.
You decide how to play them.
You're not powerless. You're not passive. You're not random.
You are **a co-creator** of your outcomes.

You learn. You fall. You rise. You evolve.
And just like the best players, you begin to realize:

The game isn't about winning.
It's about playing with presence, heart, and purpose.

So as you leave this table, remember—
You're not just a player in life.
You are the soul shaping how the story unfolds.

♠ Now go play it well.

♠ The Player's Code of Life
Wisdom for the Soul's Game

🃁 Know your worth – A poor hand doesn't mean a poor player.

🃍 Trust the turn – Even unexpected twists can bring breakthrough.

♣ Sometimes the bluff is protection, not deception – Confidence shields your process.

♦ Play the long game – Patience is a power move in both poker and purpose.

♥ Let go when it's not yours to win – Folding is a sacred act of wisdom.

♠ Read the energy, not just the table – Truth is felt before it's seen.

🂡 Your gut knows before your mind does – Intuition is your true strategy.

♣ You don't control the shuffle—but you choose how to show up – Respond, don't react.

♦ When the river hits hard, anchor in faith – Some lessons arrive in heartbreak's wake.

♥ Beginner's luck is Spirit showing off – Sometimes grace trumps skill.

♠ Tilt happens—breathe, reset, play again – Mastery includes the mess.

🃍 This isn't just a game—it's a co-creation – Your life is not random. It's divinely dealt.

BIBLIOGRAPHY

- Chopra, Deepak. *The Seven Spiritual Laws of Success.* Amber-Allen Publishing, 1994.
- Dyer, Wayne. *The Power of Intention.* Hay House, 2004.
- Gladwell, Malcolm. *Blink: The Power of Thinking Without Thinking.* Little, Brown and Company, 2005.
- Hill, Napoleon. *Think and Grow Rich.* The Ralston Society, 1937.
- Joseph, Joe. *Poker and the Meaning of Life: Discovering Wisdom at the Card Table.* Self-published, 2015.
- Jung, Carl. *Man and His Symbols.* Dell Publishing, 1964.
- Myss, Caroline. *Anatomy of the Spirit.* Harmony, 1996.
- Peale, Norman Vincent. *The Power of Positive Thinking.* Prentice Hall, 1952.
- Pressfield, Steven. *The War of Art.* Black Irish Entertainment LLC, 2002.
- RuPaul. *GuRu.* Dey Street Books, 2018.
- Santego, Constance. *Secrets of a Healer* series. Maximillian Enterprises, 2005–present.
- Tolle, Eckhart. *The Power of Now.* New World Library, 1997.
- Vanzant, Iyanla. *Acts of Faith: Daily Meditations for People of Color.* Fireside, 1993.
- Wilber, Ken. *A Brief History of Everything.* Shambhala Publications, 1996.

Additional Poker-Specific References

- Brunson, Doyle. Super System: A Course in Power Poker. Cardoza Publishing, 1979.
  – A foundational text by a poker legend; dives into strategic thinking and risk.
- Harrington, Dan. Harrington on Hold'em: Expert Strategy for No-Limit Tournaments (Vol. I–III). Two Plus Two Publishing, 2004–2006.
  – Widely respected for breaking down poker theory, mindset, and tournament logic.
- Sklansky, David. The Theory of Poker. Two Plus Two Publishing, 1994.
  – Explains core strategic principles that apply both to poker and decision-making in life.
- Tendler, Jared. The Mental Game of Poker. Jared Tendler, LLC, 2011.
  – Focuses on emotional control, mindset, and performance under pressure—very applicable to your spiritual and psychological themes.
- Hellmuth, Phil. Play Poker Like the Pros. Harper Perennial, 2003.
  – Blends confidence, intuition, and practical advice—an excellent metaphorical reference.
- St. John, Roy. Zen and the Art of Poker: Timeless Secrets to Transform Your Game. Citadel, 1999.
  – Merges poker with mindfulness, presence, and emotional regulation—perfect for your blend of life lessons and spiritual growth.

ABOUT THE AUTHOR

Dr. Constance Santego is a trailblazer in holistic health, energy medicine, and spiritual development—with more than 25 years of teaching, healing, and hands-on experience guiding thousands toward personal transformation. With a Ph.D. and Doctorate in Natural Medicine, her work is grounded in both ancient wisdom and modern understanding of the mind-body-spirit connection.

Known for her transformational teaching style, Dr. Constance Santego has empowered thousands through her workshops, trainings, and the acclaimed *Secrets of a Healer* book series. As the author of over 40 books, she explores the powerful intersections of intuition, energy medicine, metaphysics, and spiritual law—guiding readers and students on profound journeys of self-discovery. Her work invites others to reconnect with their inner truth, unlock their spiritual gifts, and live with clarity, purpose, and empowerment. Whether teaching, writing, or facilitating healing, Dr. Santego's message is unwavering: *you are your own greatest healer—and your life is not random, but intelligently guided.*

And yes—when she's not writing, teaching, or leading retreats, Dr. Santego loves to sit down at the poker table. She's been told she plays a mean game of Texas Hold'em, and truth be told... she does. Why? Because she reads energy, trusts her gut, and knows when to go all in.

This unique mix of healer and strategist is what inspired *It's Just Like Poker*—a reflection of life's risks, wins, losses, timing, and unseen magic. Just like in healing, just like in poker—how you play matters more than what you're dealt.

✧ Story Vignette – Life's a Game—But You're More Than a Player (The Author's Hand)

She'd played many hands—wife, mother, café owner, massage therapist, college director, author, spiritual guide. Some hands were blessed with aces. Others... 7–2 offsuit and no chips left on the table.

She lost people she loved. She walked away from safety. She started over more times than she could count. But she always listened—to the whispers, the gut pulls, the unseen signs. Even when no one else could hear them.

She was told she was "too much," "too intuitive," "too different."
But she kept writing. Kept teaching. Kept healing.

Her story was never about winning or losing.
It was about *alignment*.
With Spirit. With truth. With her own soul's blueprint.

And now, as she shuffles a new deck—this book in hand, this message in motion—she smiles.

Because she's not just playing the game anymore.
She's rewriting the rules.
And inviting others to join her at the table.

Message from the Author, Dr. Constance Santego

Life has dealt me a full range of hands—from heartbreak and hardship to healing and profound insight. I've sat at tables where I felt invisible… and others where I knew I was meant to lead. Through every turn of the cards, one truth has stayed constant: we're not here just to *play* the game of life—we're here to *understand* it, transform it, and teach others how to play with soul.

This book was born from years of personal experience, spiritual exploration, and deep conversations with those who—like me—felt there had to be more. More meaning. More magic. More purpose behind the pain, the detours, the gut feelings that wouldn't go away.

Whether you're holding a winning hand right now or feel like folding completely, know this: your cards do not define you. Your spirit does.

You are not alone at this table.
And you were never meant to play small.

So take a deep breath, shuffle the deck, and play from your heart.

Keep the faith,
Create your own magic,
And never forget—you're the one holding the cards.

With love and truth,
Dr. Constance Santego

ALSO AVAILABLE

Life's Poker Wisdom Deck

Intuition. Strategy. Soul.

This isn't just a card deck—it's a mirror for life. It is an oracle deck.

Inspired by the book *It's Just Like Poker* by Dr. Constance Santego, the **Life's Poker Wisdom Deck** offers 52 powerful insights that blend poker strategy with spiritual wisdom. Each card delivers a lesson in intuition, timing, risk, or emotional mastery—reminding you that life, like poker, is less about the hand you're dealt and more about how you choose to play it.

Use this deck for daily reflection, intuitive coaching, journaling prompts, or as an empowering tool in your healing practice. Whether you're facing a big decision, seeking clarity, or just need a nudge from the universe, shuffle the deck and trust what shows up.

Life's a game—but you're more than a player.
Pull a card. Play your truth.

PLAY THE GAME *IKONA* – DISCOVER YOUR INNER GENIE

For additional information on

Constance Santego's

wide range of Motivational Products, Coaching Sessions,
Spiritual Retreats,
Live Events and Educational Programs

Go to

www.ConstanceSantego.ca

Follow on Instagram - Constance_Santego and
Facebook - constancesantegoo

Subscribe and receive Free Information and Meditations on my
YouTube Channel - Constance Santego